P9-DDI-377

INDUSTRY
Transformers

The Lifetime Advantage™, The Congressional Youth Leadership Council™, The National Youth Leadership Forum™, Envision EMI™, The National Young Scholars Program™, The Junior National Young Leaders Conference™, The National Young Leaders State Conference™, The National Young Leaders Conference™, and The Global Young Leaders Conference™ are trademarks of Envision EMI, 2008. All rights reserved. Used with permission.

Jancoa® and The Facility Optimizer Process™ are trademarks of Jancoa Janitorial Services, 2008. All rights reserved. Used with permission.

The Dream Manager™ is a trademark of Floyd Consulting, Inc., 2008. All rights reserved. Used with permission.

Piranha Marketing™, The Carpet Audit™, 105 Money Making Marketing Strategies™, Elf Marketing™, and The Genius Network™ are trademarks of Piranha Marketing, Inc., 2008. All rights reserved. Used with permission.

7 Steps to a 720® Credit Score and 7 Steps to 720® are trademarks of 7 Steps to 720, LLC., 2008. All rights reserved. Used with permission.

The Boomer Technology Circles™, The Performance^{3}™ Formula, The Boomer Advantage Guides™, and The Performance^{3}™ Management Program™ are trademarks of Boomer Consulting, Inc., 2008. All rights reserved. Used with permission.

The Allen Groupe Experience™ The Pre-Flight Discovery™, The Flight Plan™, The Autopilot Navigator™, The Allen Groupe Difference™, and The Post-Flight Debrief™ are trademarks of The Allen Groupe, 2008. All rights reserved. Used with permission.

TM & © 2008, 2015. The Strategic Coach Inc. All rights reserved.

No part of this work may be reproduced in any form, or by any means whatsoever, without written permission from The Strategic Coach Inc., except in the case of brief quotations embodied in critical articles and reviews.

Printed in Toronto, Canada. March 2015. The Strategic Coach Inc., 33 Fraser Avenue, Suite 201, Toronto, Ontario, M6K 3J9.

This publication is meant to strengthen your common sense, not to substitute for it. It is also not a substitute for the advice of your doctor, lawyer, accountant, or any of your advisors, personal or professional.

Library and Archives Canada Cataloguing in Publication

Sullivan, Dan, 1944-
        Industry transformers / Dan Sullivan.

ISBN 978-1-897239-14-8

        1. Success in business. 2. Entrepreneurship. 3. Businesspeople--Biography.
I. Title.

Contents

Two Exciting Ideas

Foreword

A brief explanation of two exciting ideas.

The following pages are filled with exciting stories and ideas. Two of the most important concepts I will introduce are the idea of a "Unique Process entrepreneur" and the idea of an "Industry Transformer." Each represents a new way for successful and ambitious entrepreneurs to develop and expand in today's fast-changing marketplace. Here is a brief explanation of these two ideas.

Unique Process™ entrepreneurs.
In 1804, a French economist, Jean-Baptiste Say, defined an entrepreneur as *someone who takes resources from a lower to a higher level of productivity.* It was a good definition two centuries ago, and it's an even better one today. In every industry, entrepreneurs are those who create new breakthroughs in getting things done faster and better than larger, slower moving, less responsive organizations. In some cases, they create entirely new kinds of economic activity, results, and value. The Austrian economist Joseph Schumpeter believed that entrepreneurs are the ones who introduce "creative destruction" into human affairs. By this he meant that entrepreneurs, by continually creating new ways of getting things done, are responsible for the emergence of new, better, and different kinds of communication, cooperation, and creativity. In the process of being creative, they continually destroy less productive, "status quo" arrangements, relationships, and institutions in all indus-

tries and markets. The last 25 years have certainly seen great evidence of this entrepreneurially-induced creative destruction occurring in every sector.

The entrepreneurs who cause the greatest creative destruction over the long run are those who operate within Unique Processes. These are custom-designed businesses that combine two ingredients: the Unique Ability* of the individual entrepreneur and the unique dangers, opportunities, and strengths of their specific clientele. The creative combination of these two elements drives a self-evolving process of problem solving that provides more powerful and satisfying results for the clientele, and greater revenues and profits for the entrepreneur. Because each component of the process is truly unique—and understandable only from the inside—the resulting entrepreneurial company becomes more and more immune to competition in its marketplace. *Unique Process entrepreneurs enjoy continually growing business and personal advantages that are not attainable by other entrepreneurs who do not operate within a Unique Process.*

Industry Transformers.
As Unique Process entrepreneurs grow their revenues and profits, and as the positive reputation of their uniquely valuable problem solving spreads throughout the marketplace, they increasingly transform the structures, relationships, and institutions of their industry. They become a powerful force of creative destruction. Their competitors, noticing their extraordinary success, try various means of keeping pace to no avail. Gradually, a new industry begins to emerge as more clients, capital, and talent gravitate to the Unique Process entrepreneur's new way of doing business. This transformation from the status quo to the new model accelerates over time. And all because a single entrepreneur did things in a new, better way.

* For the definition of Unique Ability, please see page 212.

Industry Transformers

Industry Transformers

A U.S. senator's aide and a committed school teacher from Connecticut create an alternative educational system that transforms the attitudes and ambitions of hundreds of thousands of the best and brightest students from the U.S. and abroad.

A husband-and-wife partnership in Cincinnati transforms a janitorial company into a think-tank for industry innovations and also into a national organizational model that enables immigrant workers to become successful, upwardly mobile U.S. citizens and homeowners.

A patent attorney from Silicon Valley, faced with a 90 percent drop in fees caused by recession and outsourcing, develops an integrative positioning-and-protection strategy that helps startup technology companies to become monopoly enterprises.

A carpet cleaner in Phoenix develops an extraordinary marketing system that transforms the profitability and professionalism of thousands of other firms in his industry—then goes on to apply the same system to dozens of other industries.

A mortgage broker in Santa Monica develops a seven-step educational process that enables thousands of people to save millions by having higher credit scores, then packages his wisdom so that thousands of other brokers in the U.S. can help their customers do the same.

An entrepreneur in Omaha takes over a nearly-bankrupt company and transforms it into a national "matchmaking" network that is now responsible for millions of American high school students finding the right college for themselves among thousands of institutions.

An accountant in Kansas gives up his practice to create a cutting-edge coaching system that enables hundreds of successful accounting firms to utilize technological breakthroughs to increase productivity and profitability.

A car washer from Indianapolis teaches himself how to clean private airplanes, then creates a "detailing" approach that goes on to dominate the private jet industry worldwide.

Unique Process entrepreneurs who transform industries. This book describes how eight entrepreneurial companies in different industries have capitalized on a single business structure called a Unique Process to become extraordinarily productive and profitable, with the result that they are continually transforming their industries. By transforming themselves into value creation enterprises, they have become role models and teachers for many other companies.

The creators of these Unique Processes are all participants in the Strategic Coach® Program, a lifetime focusing program for highly successful entrepreneurs. The promise of Strategic Coach® is "lifetime growth" for entrepreneurs in all areas of their lives. The Unique Process is one of the key concepts of the Program, and makes lifetime growth not only an exciting promise but, as you will read in these pages, a practical and permanent reality for any entrepreneur who has the desire to create a "value creation monopoly" in his or her marketplace.

Having a value creation monopoly creates extraordinary personal and professional freedom.
Achieving this monopoly through the power of a Unique Process is an extraordinary advantage. There is no other business strategy that compares with it. Having a value creation monopoly introduces entrepreneurs to ever-increasing levels of professional and personal freedom that are beyond the comprehension of business owners who do not have a Unique Process. Unique Process entrepreneurs can plan, prepare, and execute in a continually innovative fashion that produces bigger, better, and more satisfying results. The increased freedom of thinking, decision making, and action makes the investment, hard work, and risk taking of being an entrepreneur worthwhile. It makes each day's activities exciting, and makes being an entrepreneur enjoyable for a lifetime.

The value creation monopoly, based on a creative partnership with clients and customers, essentially frees Unique Process entrepreneurs from the forces of commoditization that make life anxious, difficult, and frustrating for those who do not utilize this concept and have not built their businesses around this structure.

The entrepreneurial benefits of having a Unique Process.
Strategic Coach, the innovator and developer of the Unique Process approach, has coached well over 10,000 entrepreneurs at its centers in the U.S., Canada, and the U.K. The company itself has been a Unique Process enterprise for the past 25 years and has achieved its own value creation monopoly in the entrepreneurial marketplace. In other words, in writing this book, I am preaching what my company has been successfully practicing since the early 1980s. The result is that we are widely recognized as the premier coaching company for successful entrepreneurs.

My wife, Babs Smith, and I are the founders and owners of a company whose central goal is to help thousands of other entrepreneurs create their own Unique Process companies. By doing this, we hope there will be a growing global community of enterprises that share the same transformative philosophy, methodology, and extraordinary results. The eight interviews in this book demonstrate the qualities, capabilities, and ambitions of the hundreds of entrepreneurial companies that are already part of this Unique Process community. My purpose in writing this book is to invite many other entrepreneurs to be inspired and motivated by these success stories, and then to take the steps to transform their companies so that they can join this community.

There are many benefits that come from doing so. Here are a few that I have noticed over the past decade from watching the progress of our clients' Unique Process companies. Unique Process entrepreneurs:

- Differentiate themselves from all existing and would-be competitors in their industry in ways that are positive, appealing, impactful, and permanent.

- Establish long-term growth relationships with their clients and customers, who become their greatest sales force.

- Get paid extra, and upfront, for their unique wisdom, innovation, and problem-solving capabilities.

- Protect their products and services from being commoditized.

- Attract high-quality team members and associates who become long-term creative team members within the Unique Process organization.

- Achieve higher levels of productivity and profitability on an ongoing basis.

- Continually innovate new business concepts, tools, and systems that always keep them on the cutting edge of progress and successes.

- Achieve value creation monopolies in every area of their activities, with a constantly increasing impact and influence in their marketplace and industry.

- Develop proprietary "intellectual capital" that continually increases the market value of their companies.

- Position and package themselves and their businesses as "intellectual capital companies."

The inner ingredients of Industry Transformer™ success.
The eight entrepreneurial companies that are featured in this book are all enjoying these benefits, and will continue to strengthen them in the future. But these benefits are the result of much deeper principles and strategies at work. In studying these and other entrepreneurial successes in our Unique Process community, we have identified eight ingredients that, over time, transform these companies into Industry Transformers. As you will learn from the interviews that follow, none of these business owners set out to transform their industry. Nor in many cases does it particularly excite them when it is pointed out that they are doing so. For them, being an Industry Transformer is simply a by-product of pursuing more important purposes in their work.

The nine entrepreneurs we interviewed set out to improve their personal and professional lives, to be more useful to their clientele, and to increase their entrepreneurial freedom. We have discovered that when you pursue these objectives within the structure of a Unique Process, you naturally and invariably begin to gain all of the benefits outlined above. *And you automatically begin to transform, for the better, the industry in which you are operating.*

I have organized the body of the book into interviews and "ingredients." In the interviews, I asked the entrepreneurs to tell the stories of their entrepreneurial lives and to focus on the success of their Unique Process businesses. In the Ingredients sections, I have highlighted eight factors that seem to have most contributed to their Unique Process successes. This has been a labor of love on my part. My passion in my business and in life is to see talented and creative entrepreneurs transform every part of their personal and professional lives on an accelerating basis. It was very gratifying, therefore, to hear how these Unique Process entrepreneurs are achieving this.

Overcoming Adversity

Overcoming Adversity

One of the more noticeable common traits of the individuals featured in this book is the personal transformation of adversity of one kind or another. It seems that the challenge of overcoming obstacles, deficiencies, and shortcomings in their own lives has led to a growing lifetime capability to transform the situations of other people.

In some cases, the adversity that needed to be overcome was a lack of funding. Don Munce, in his interview, recounts how he needed to secure a million dollars virtually overnight to avoid bankruptcy.

In other cases, the entrepreneurs had to face their own lack of experience, knowledge, and skill. David Allen tells the story of his early years in the jet-cleaning business, working body-destroying hours with no strategy or plan, where every day's efforts were costing him "fourteen dollars to make ten."

Some, they admit to chaotic personal lives, disabilities, addictions, and wrong-headedness. Tony Miller described how he made it halfway through grade school without being able to read, and later had to come to grips with the sudden loss of his father, and with his own alcoholism.

Unexpected changes in the marketplace were yet another source of setbacks. John Ferrell describes how, in 2003, the fees his firm could charge for patents, a main source of cash flow and profits, suddenly fell from $15,000 to $1,500 in six months.

Almost all of them laugh at these things now, but the situations weren't amusing when they were dealing with them. What is notable, however, is that, regardless of their experiences, all of these entrepreneurs had what I call a "transformative attitude" about themselves and their lives. In every case, they used the adversity or obstacles as "raw material" for personal growth, progress, achievement, and success. Having done this for themselves, they turned the lesson of their personal experiences into a business approach. Having successfully faced difficult situations themselves, they began looking for the difficult situations that others were facing. Having grown stronger and more skillful by overcoming adversity in their own businesses, they identified new areas of value creation in the adversity of other people's businesses and lives. They transformed their own dangers into opportunities, and their own deficiencies into strengths. They treated, and continue to treat, the difficulties of their own lives as a continual training school for becoming more useful to others.

The transformative attitude differentiates entrepreneurs.
Having personally coached more than six thousand entrepreneurs over the past 30 years, I believe that this transformative attitude is in large part what differentiates entrepreneurs from the general population. Other people are stopped or frightened off by adversity; entrepreneurs aren't. Other people are stopped by their obstacles, but entrepreneurs seem to gain positive benefits and advantages from dealing with theirs. But even among entrepreneurs, there are those who continually transform themselves and their situations much more purposefully and successfully. The entrepreneurs featured here —like Don Munce, Joe Polish, and Tony Miller—are at the far

positive end of the spectrum. Because I have known each of these entrepreneurs for more than ten years, I can state the following about all of them:

- They treat deficiencies in themselves and their organizations as invitations to grow.

- They treat obstacles and opposition as opportunities to change their thinking and methods.

- They treat failures, breakdowns, and setbacks as opportunities to learn and improve.

- They treat their uncertainty, anxiety, and fear as fuel for personal achievement.

- They treat sudden changes in the marketplace as opportunities to create new value for others and advantages for themselves.

- They treat their own weaknesses as opportunities to utilize the strengths of others.

As you can readily see, these are not the normal ways of thinking, responding, and acting for many people today. There is no room for complaining here. None for criticizing others. No room for blaming. None for self-pity or making excuses. What there is, instead, is a powerful self-responsibility that sees life as a school, and all of life's experiences, especially the scariest and most difficult ones, as valuable tests and lessons. My sense is that Don, Joe, and Tony, and the others featured here, had these attitudes and qualities long before they became entrepreneurs. They became entrepreneurs because they already had them. For whatever reason, from an early age, they learned how to overcome adversity in their personal lives.

Where others stopped in the face of opposition and shied away from adversity, they chose to keep moving and make friends with difficulty. *They chose an entrepreneurial path because they already possessed the mental toughness and agility needed to deal with the kinds of challenges that entrepreneurs face.* Being an entrepreneur for many years has only deepened and expanded these capabilities in each of them.

Overcoming adversity, then, is the first key ingredient of becoming a Unique Process entrepreneur and an Industry Transformer. Our first interview is with Richard Rossi who, as he puts it, was a "lowly aide" to a U.S. senator. One of his jobs in this position was to handle requests from the senator's constituents, among them a very demanding Connecticut school teacher named Barbara Harris. An elected official in Washington, especially a senator, gets hundreds of requests per day. The staff is always overburdened with work. Richard could have responded to her unrelenting requests for special treatment for her students in a number of different ways. He could have done the minimum. He could have tried to pass her off to someone else. He could have explained that there was only so much that any senator's office could do for her and tried to change her way of thinking. Instead of doing any of these, he took the approach of providing absolutely the best support that the office could provide. He provided her with first-class experiences for all of her students. In doing so, he helped create the opportunity of a lifetime, for both himself and for Barbara.

Richard Rossi

The Lifetime Advantage™

As a young aide to a U.S. senator, Richard Rossi was assigned to help one of his constituents, Barbara Harris — the type of passionate teacher that every parent hopes their child will have — organize the stellar Washington, D.C., field trip she had in mind for her students. Emboldened by their success and seeing an opportunity to provide a life-changing leadership experience to thousands of exceptional students from around the world, the two founded Envision EMI in Vienna, Virginia, and created a Unique Process, The Lifetime Advantage™, to fulfill their exciting and extraordinary

Dan Sullivan: It's great to be talking with you, Richard. Before we start, one thing I want to recognize is that your co-founder, Barbara Harris, wasn't able to be with us today. So why don't you tell us a little about how you met Barbara and how the seeds were planted for this extraordinary collaboration.

Richard Rossi: Certainly none of this would have happened without Barbara, so I'll just include her in everything we discuss. Back in the mid-1970s I was in my mid-twenties and working as an aide to Lowell Weicker, a U.S. senator from Connecticut. Barbara was in her mid-fifties, working as a schoolteacher in Ridgefield, Connecticut.

Dan Sullivan: Sounds like an unlikely pairing.

Richard Rossi: I guess it might appear that way. But, actually, my job in the senator's office was to deal with people like Barbara. Barbara was what we'd call a troublesome constituent. She was one of those folks who would call the senator's office and say, "Listen, I am coming to Washington with a group of high school students. This isn't going to be just any old tour. I actually want every student in the group to have an individual experience that's customized to their interests. If there's a young person who wants to be a zoologist, they'll spend a day at the National Zoo; if they want to go into astronomy, they'll go to the Goddard Space Flight Center; medicine, they'll go to the National Institutes of Health. I want Senator Weicker and Senator Weicker's staff to make these things happen for me as a constituent of Connecticut."

Dan Sullivan: *How did the senator's office usually deal with people like that?*
Richard Rossi: Well, they're usually just passed down the line to those in the office who are the youngest and most inexperienced, so of course I got the case. We met over the phone. And I realized that Barbara was one of those teachers that you'd want your children to have. Her whole purpose was to try and provide enriching experiences for the young people that were placed in her care. One thing I learned is that Barbara just doesn't take no for an answer, and that remains true to this day.

Dan Sullivan: *So you were able to help her.*
Richard Rossi: Yes, I was. We sort of became friends, and every year she brought a class down. Then the time came for President Reagan's first inauguration. She wanted to bring a small group of students down, and we managed to rustle up enough tickets for the ball, the parade, and the actual swearing-in.

Dan Sullivan: *I bet the students had a blast.*
Richard Rossi: They sure did. So fast-forward to Reagan's second inauguration in January 1985. By then I had left the senator's office to start my own business. At first, I focused on providing computer services to political campaigns, but this wasn't going anywhere. Then Barbara, God bless her, caught Potomac Fever. She decided to leave her career as a teacher and school administrator to come to Washington and

seek her fortune. She was going to create programs for members of Congress, where they could bring their constituents to Washington and enjoy the same experience that Barbara was so good at creating for her students.

Dan Sullivan: *How did you connect?*
Richard Rossi: She called me up, and I offered her some office space down the hall. Then one day, she came to me and said, "Richard, what do you think about trying to bring a group of young people to Washington to take part in the inauguration?" We talked it over and hatched the idea over the table in one day. I had gained some direct-marketing experience working for the Republican Party, and we decided to send a mailing to principals around the country urging them to nominate their best student to come to this inauguration. It was just a sole proprietorship, and we called it The Election 84 Youth Inaugural Conference.

Dan Sullivan: *You had nothing to lose.*
Richard Rossi: Exactly. And the idea took off. We sent letters to all 535 members of Congress asking them to join our Honorary Board of Advisors. Ninety-three of them agreed. We sent the mailing out to principals around the country, and, long story short, it was a very, very big success. A few days before the inauguration we walked into a hotel ballroom in Alexandria, Virginia, and there were over 400 young people sitting there in ties, jackets, and dresses.

Dan Sullivan: *And just totally excited.*
Richard Rossi: Totally excited. You know, we had been so busy upstairs preparing that we hadn't even been part of the arrivals. We came downstairs and were just totally blown away by the energy in the room. It ended up being a great experience for the kids. We managed to rustle up 400 tickets to the Inaugural Ball,

and we also took them to other events around Washington, some of which are still part of our programs today. Certainly, there was no reason to believe this would be successful. We each put a few thousand dollars in and got family and friends to volunteer, so it was actually quite profitable. Throughout the process we were pretty relaxed. After all, what's the worst that could happen? Barbara would go back to being a schoolteacher.

Dan Sullivan: *And you'd be banned from Washington.*
Richard Rossi: (Laughing) Fortunately, that didn't happen.

Dan Sullivan: *Richard, I have a question. You've given us a vivid picture of Barbara's passion for her students. When did you start developing that same passion for helping young people succeed?*
Richard Rossi: For me, from the beginning, it was just an interesting business opportunity. Only after the programs started catching on did I get that fire for helping young people reach their potential.

Dan Sullivan: *So we're in 1985, and you've just had a successful event. What was your next step?*
Richard Rossi: Well, shortly thereafter, Barbara and I got the idea of trying to make a larger business out of this process of bringing young people around the country together to learn about citizenship and democracy and leadership. So we founded The Congressional Youth Leadership Council™. Once again, we did a mailing, and it was successful. I have to emphasize that at no point did we have any money, capital, or resources. We did this whole thing on a wing and a prayer. There was no fall-back position. We were very lucky it worked out.

Dan Sullivan: *As you progressed, what kinds of insights were you getting about this type of business?*

Richard Rossi: We discovered, first of all, that we were doing a great job selling, and also that our programs were extremely well received by the young people and their parents. We had parents who would call and say, "Who is this person that you've sent back to me? They're so much more confident. They're so much more interested in their future and in their country's democratic process." It really was perceived as a transformative experience for their son or daughter.

Dan Sullivan: *You probably had some champions among the principals too.*
Richard Rossi: What actually happened is we started shifting our marketing away from principals and toward teachers. We found that principals are often bureaucratic and looking for a reason to say no. Teachers, on the other hand, have this real affection for their students.

Dan Sullivan: *There are a lot of Barbaras out there.*
Richard Rossi: The teachers just want what's best for their students, so they've always been our biggest champions.

Dan Sullivan: *What was the next growth juncture?*
Richard Rossi: Well we were continuing to grow the Congressional Youth Leadership Council, but we realized that there's a real clamoring out there for programs that teach people about career interests. So in 1992, we founded The National Youth Leadership Forum™, which is a tuition-based educational program that helps prepare highly talented young people for their professional career. The program has taken off, and we now have forums on national security professions, law professions, and medical professions. It's come to the point where everybody knows us in the military establishment, and the Pentagon now has a manual prepared on how to take care of our program each year.

Dan Sullivan: *It's become institutionalized.*

Richard Rossi: Exactly, and I can tell you it was hard to get in the door with a big bureaucracy like the Pentagon, but once you're in, you tend to stay in. The medical program has also taken off, and we're now in nine cities, with over 8,000 young people attending each year.

Dan Sullivan: *Why don't we shift gears a little and talk about your company, Envision EMI™, because I know it's been very important in terms of supporting the growth of these programs?*

Richard Rossi: Sure. Envision EMI is basically the umbrella company that administers all the different programs in our portfolio. You know, when we first started out, Barbara and I weren't very organized. I can't even begin to tell you how rinky-dink the whole thing was. We had tiny offices and only one computer, so people had to sign up in shifts to use it. We didn't keep records or mailing addresses of people who attended.

Dan Sullivan: *You needed an organization to support your ambition.*

Richard Rossi: Exactly. And over time, we've built our company, Envision EMI, into a really powerful Unique Ability Team* with over 200 full-time employees. At any one time, we might have 1,000 part-time people. This team is responsible for administering all the programs, doing the marketing, finding the participants. I must tell you that a watershed moment for the company was when I joined Strategic Coach. Up until that time, Barbara and I weren't really used to thinking in terms of big goals. We were always focusing on the day-to-day minutiae, still interviewing every employee and signing every check.

Dan Sullivan: *You were 24/7 guys.*

Richard Rossi: Unfortunately, yes. But when we joined the Coach, we started asking, "How big can our future be?" And we knew there was just a lot more room for growth.

Dan Sullivan: *Can you talk a little about how Envision EMI is structured?*
Richard Rossi: Sure. We have different teams. So one is involved in recruiting, and another is focused on delivering a great educational experience. The education folks are split into two parts. First, there are those who create the actual curriculum—materials, books, lesson plans. The other part includes those who actually have to put the show on and recruit the hundreds of temporary staff we hire each year. These are the program directors who oversee the temporary staff. But everyone is focused on the same core objectives, which are captured by our company mission statement: "Educate, motivate, inspire."

Dan Sullivan: *What an enormous undertaking.*
Richard Rossi: Fortunately, we've developed hundreds of specific methods over the years, the majority of which Barbara and I don't even really know about, because we have great people working for us who oversee all of that. My role in the company is very forward-thinking. I don't do anything that involves day-to-day operations. Obviously, Barbara and I approve the overall strategy and the annual budget, but beyond that we're really thinking about how to grow our business exponentially.

Dan Sullivan: *Sitting here in 2008, what's the scope of your offerings?*
Richard Rossi: Well, we start with second-, third-, fourth-, and fifth-graders through a program called The National Young Scholars Program™. For sixth- and seventh-grade students, we have something called The Junior National Young

* For the definition of Unique Ability Team, please see page 212.

■ *If there's one overarching theme in all of our programs, it's leadership. We want to give young people a lifetime edge that can help them achieve their full potential.* ■

Leaders Conference™ that brings young people to Washington to study leadership through historical role models. They go to Harpers Ferry, they go to Colonial Williamsburg, they go to Capitol Hill, and it's just a spectacular experience. For ninth- graders, we have The National Young Leaders State Conference™. The participants actually stay in a hotel room for three or four days and study personal leadership skills like goal setting, confidence building, communication, negotiation, and time management. These are the kinds of things most people learn later in life and say, "Gee, I wish I'd learned that 20 years ago."

Dan Sullivan: *All of these programs are part of the Congressional Youth Leadership Council umbrella.*
Richard Rossi: Exactly. The next program, starting in Grade 10, is The National Young Leaders Conference™, and this is our major conference for high school students. Then we have The Global Young Leaders Conference™, which brings people from over 100 different countries to Washington and New York to study globalization, democracy, and diplomacy. Participants might visit places like the Department of State and the United Nations. They'll attend museums like the Smithsonian, while being exposed to issues affecting the global economy and international business. So it's a really comprehensive program. We offer a version of the program in Europe as well. Finally, we have a program for the college market that has college students visit a variety of different foreign countries to study specific career interests.

Dan Sullivan: *So you basically have a continuum of offerings from third grade all the way through the college level.*

Richard Rossi: That's the idea. We finally have a product line that can attract and retain long-term, repeat customers as their children progress through the education system. We also have young people who have been through our programs and will come back to work for Envision EMI, which is very gratifying. If there's one overarching theme in all of our programs, it's leadership. We want to give young people a lifetime edge that can help them achieve their full potential.

Dan Sullivan: *How many young people are going through your programs each year?*

Richard Rossi: I'd estimate about 50,000 per year, which means that over the past 22 years, close to half a million young people have been through our programs.

Dan Sullivan: *That's really a staggering number, Richard. If you're talking about a single high school, not only is that far greater than the student body, it's significantly greater than the total number of alumni who have ever graduated from that school.*

Richard Rossi: That's a nice way of capturing it. But what really makes us unique is that we only focus on the best and the brightest. This makes our job a lot easier. The students are already so talented and so motivated that they can really take advantage of our programs. And the parents recognize this talent so they're extremely enthusiastic about sending their kids.

Dan Sullivan: *Richard, some of your earliest participants are now in their thirties. Do they ever come back and talk to you?*

Richard Rossi: They do come back, and what always stands out are the friendships they've developed with fellow participants and faculty advisors. The impact of the program is ongoing—it doesn't end when the program ends.

Dan Sullivan: *You must have a pretty high insurance liability, dealing with all of these talented young people.*
Richard Rossi: One of my friends was an insurance executive, and I remember asking him about our liability. He basically said it's unlimited. We've got busloads of America's best and brightest seventeen-year-olds, and if something unspeakable were to happen, we're really in a vulnerable position. So it's one of the issues Envision EMI constantly has to look out for, making sure our programs are top-notch from a safety and logistical standpoint.

Dan Sullivan: *Of course, one of the things that differentiates Envision EMI from a lot of other organizations running educational programs is that you're operating on a for-profit basis. How has that incentive structure influenced your ability to innovate and create value in the marketplace?*
Richard Rossi: That's a great question, Dan. When we first started out, some programs were organized as non-profits with independent boards of directors because it just wasn't acceptable to do it any other way. We certainly wouldn't have enjoyed the same broad political support in Washington if these programs didn't start out as independent non-profits. Twenty years ago, there was just a different set of stan-

What parents and teachers are looking for is a high-quality program that can have a transformative impact on students, and that's certainly what we deliver.

dards. Now we see for-profit companies like the University of Phoenix, along with test prep companies and college counseling services. All of these businesses are challenging the old taboo, which assumed that anybody paying taxes in the education world was illegitimate or unethical.

Dan Sullivan: *At the present time, all of your major programs are for-profit, right?*
Richard Rossi: Yes. We've always had a balance between for-profit and non-profit but we're now in the process of purchasing the assets of The Congressional Youth Leadership Council and The National Youth Leadership Forum. Now it's come to the point where people really don't care about that distinction. What parents and teachers are looking for is a high-quality program that can have a transformative impact on students, and that's certainly what we deliver.

Dan Sullivan: *I also presume that despite this shift, you continue to get a good reception from the Washington establishment. Why don't you talk a bit about the attitude of public officials and other honorary figures toward your programs? I know a lot of prominent people sit on the Congressional Youth Leadership Council board and you invite a lot of these people to speak in front of student groups.*
Richard Rossi: First of all, everyone loves to be admired. Yet no matter what we say, their expectations are usually low. "These are high school students. Well, all right, I'll do this appearance once and that will be that." Then they walk into a room full of young people sitting respectfully, dressed in ties and jackets or dresses for the ladies. They're so smart, so interested, so admiring, and the questions are so insightful, that when the event ends the speaker comes to us and says, "Wow, I just love this, and I'm happy to help." They're blown away by the level of engagement and intensity in the room,

*Experiential education is a huge market ...
we're not even close to maxing out our potential.
Barbara and I are always asking, "What's the
next big thing?"*

and it energizes them to stay involved. That's why I always say that our real secret is in the selection process. The real secret is in our ability to continually attract the best and brightest.

Dan Sullivan: *Speaking of the best and brightest, it's very interesting to see how you've decided to approach the education of your own children. Why don't you talk a bit about that?*
Richard Rossi: Sure. I'm just a huge believer in experiential education, and I have issues with the traditional school system. My wife and I don't have the Unique Ability® to teach the children ourselves, so we actually bought a house in the D.C. area and converted it into a schoolhouse for both of our kids. We hired a teacher and worked with her to create a curriculum. We make sure to incorporate a lot of real-life experiences into the curriculum. And we're certainly lucky to live in the D.C. area, which is an unbelievable classroom—the Smithsonian alone.

Dan Sullivan: *At a broader level, of course, you're not only transforming your children's education. Your programs are also transforming the whole education industry by turning this idea of experiential education into a Unique Process that supports an entire organization and all of the programs you've talked about today.*
Richard Rossi: I believe that you're right, and I say that humbly, but I don't think the facts can lead you to any other conclusion. All too often, in the traditional education system,

Richard Rossi

the high achiever gets ignored. The institutional focus is always on teaching to the test and dealing with basic competencies. In contrast, we celebrate the high achievers and provide an innovative atmosphere where they can grow.

Dan Sullivan: *Just looking at the capabilities and methods you've developed, there really isn't any stopping point. You're just scratching the surface.*
Richard Rossi: That's very true. Experiential education is a huge market, and it's only a matter of what part of the market we can get. But we're not even close to maxing out our potential. Barbara and I are always asking, "What's the next big thing?" Certainly Strategic Coach has been a really important influence in terms of helping us think big. I truly appreciate everything that the entire Strategic Coach team has done for us.

Dan Sullivan: *Thanks, Richard. Now, I want to return to something we discussed earlier, and that's your passion for helping young people. I know at the beginning you primarily viewed this as a business opportunity, but sitting here now, with the way everything has taken off, you must feel an enormous amount of passion and pride in what you're doing to transform the education industry.*
Richard Rossi: That passion became very prominent during the mid-1990s, when I realized that our programs were actually having an impact on the future of the world. They weren't just vehicles for growing our company financially. They had become far, far bigger than me or any other individual. Some of my happiest moments are when Barbara and I are out in the field spending time with the program, observing the program. Whenever I go out and spend time in the field, that passion just rekindles.

Dan Sullivan: *Richard, I understand that several years ago, you took your wife and kids on a once-in-a-lifetime trip around the world. I think our readers would love to hear more about this adventure, especially because one of the themes we want to emphasize is the extraordinary set of personal rewards available to people like you who have built their business and gone down the road to industry transformation.*

Richard Rossi: This is a topic I can spend hours talking about, Dan, so I'll try and restrain myself. I think it was more than 12 years ago when I first told my wife that when we had kids, I wanted to take them around the world and give them a sense of how beautiful and fragile the world is. This was a dream of mine for years, and as the business became more and more successful, I started to think, "Hey, we can actually do this." It took several years to plan the trip, and then we ended up traveling for more than six months, spread out over a nine-month period of time. We visited all seven continents and went on something like 65 different plane rides. We even created a website, *www.lifesgreatestadventure.com.*

Dan Sullivan: *How old were your kids at the time?*

Richard Rossi: One was twelve and the other was ten. But this wasn't one of those "let's go and see what happens" trips. We hired a tutor who worked with us from Washington and developed an integrated curriculum that corresponded to each site we were visiting. So this allowed the children to compare and contrast the various cultures we encountered and their approach to things like religion and social life.

Dan Sullivan: *I'm sure a lot of entrepreneurs out there can't even imagine leaving their business for six months. So it's a real testament to your accomplishments that you had an organization in place that could allow you to leave without skipping a beat.*

Richard Rossi: Thanks, Dan. You know, I can count on one hand the number of times I checked in with work during the trip. I was just totally confident in our team at Envision EMI, and when I came home, there really weren't a lot of messes to clean up. So it was an extraordinary feeling to know that I have this freedom to pursue some of my dreams in life without jeopardizing the business.

Dan Sullivan: Richard, you've created a huge, transformational experience for half a million people. But one of the things I've discovered is that in the process of creating a business, entrepreneurs essentially create a school to transform themselves. What kind of transformation has Richard Rossi gone through over the past 22 years?

Richard Rossi: That's a great question. I think the big transformation for me has been in understanding my life's purpose. For a long time, my objective was simply to be successful financially and build a great business. I never saw myself as someone who could have a larger impact on humanity. Now I really feel that sense of purpose. I feel so blessed to know that I'm not just out there making widgets. I'm actually in a position to do well financially by doing good in the world.

For contact details on The Lifetime Advantage, please see page 216.

INGREDIENT 2

Passion

Ingredient 2

Passion

Every transformation of an industry starts with an overriding passion on the part of a single entrepreneur. In the case of Barbara Harris and Richard Rossi, it was the passion to have the best and brightest students have learning experiences and challenges that were equal to their capabilities and ambitions.

This passion, as we see with these two individuals, is the permanent, lifetime love of something. In the case of Gary Boomer, it was a love of using technological capabilities to increase productivity and profitability—and to share his insights with other firms and practitioners in the accounting industry.

As we will also see, the "something" that is loved, that is the source of the passion, can be anything. For example, Tony and Mary Miller have a passion for transforming the situations and fortunes of their employees and their families. Through their Dream Manager process, they are helping thousands of people in what could be "dead-end" jobs plot out and implement a lifetime of personal progress within the American economy and society.

In the case of almost every entrepreneur we explored for this book, the passion is focused on crucial improvements in the way that other people are able to live their lives. For Philip Tirone, the passion lies in enabling tens of millions of Americans to gain maximum use of their money by learning how to achieve and maintain high credit scores.

Transformation results from an "others-focused" passion.
We have also discovered that the passion is almost never
about the personal advancement or aggrandizement of the
entrepreneurs themselves. In David Allen's case, he designed
cutting-edge software for his biggest customer, NetJets, then
shared the advantages of this breakthrough with his competitors. As David put it, *"Look, it takes the productivity and
professionalism of everyone up a notch. Whether the client
is working with us or our competitors, this tool makes things
better for everyone. Besides, the word has gone around.
Everybody knows who created it."*

In this sense, the entrepreneurial passion that is powerful
enough to transform industries is always "others-focused."
Don Munce is passionate about high school students and their
parents having the best possible information to make the right
college choice. On the other hand, he is just as passionate
about colleges and universities locating and communicating
with high-quality students. His company does extraordinarily
well, Don is financially well off, and he has a great lifestyle. But
in talking with him, what he is always most excited about are
the breakthroughs that he and his team are creating for their
clients.

In each case of industry transformation, the entrepreneur is
passionate about making a crucial, lasting, positive impact on
actual clients and customers in the marketplace that is available
to them. This passionate desire to be permanently useful lies at
the core of their personal meaning as individuals, and it keeps
getting stronger.

In Strategic Coach, we have hundreds of entrepreneurs operating inside their Unique Processes. Some have been doing so
for years, while others are in the early stages. Many more are
getting ready to start the journey. I have noticed that the progress these entrepreneurs make and the success they enjoy is

first and foremost a function of the passion they bring to the project. They already have the prime ingredient of passion; Strategic Coach provides the structure for them to maximize it. The Unique Process speeds up the progress and success of these entrepreneurs because it frees up and channels their lifetime passion to be useful in extraordinarily valuable and rewarding ways.

Qualities of entrepreneurs with a passion to be useful.
Not all entrepreneurs in the marketplace have this passion to be useful. Some are strictly looking out for themselves. But this quickly becomes apparent, making it easy to identify the ones who are truly looking out for others. The latter have the following four qualities:

- Their greatest enjoyment comes from helping other people gain greater clarity, confidence, and capability.

- Their greatest satisfaction comes from seeing other people succeed as a result of their wisdom and skill.

- Their greatest meaning comes from knowing they have made a permanent, crucial difference in the growth, progress, and success of others.

- Their greatest purpose lies in developing new capabilities of their own that will be useful to an even greater number of people.

A greater number of passionately useful entrepreneurs.
These qualities are obviously not present in all entrepreneurs, but I see them in a growing number of those who join Strategic Coach. I'm not entirely sure of all the reasons for the increase, but several factors seem to be at play. Technology is certainly one. Today's computer-based tools, systems, and networks make it much easier for single, technology-savvy entrepreneurs

to have a big impact in the marketplace than was true even ten years ago. Another factor is abundance, both of money and opportunity. Consumers in every industry have a universe of choices that keeps growing. Consumption, for many people, is no longer about basic necessities. More and more, it's about personal expression and self-determination. Many more people have the resources to lead custom-designed lives, with special-ized needs, wants, and desires, than ever before. This opens up many opportunities for entrepreneurs to create and cultivate specialized market niches. The entrepreneurs best able to do this are those who have a passion for creating and providing particular types of solutions in new marketplaces. The most successful have the four qualities of being passionately useful.

A great example of two such entrepreneurs is Tony and Mary Miller, who have transformed their janitorial company into a platform for innovations that are improving lives and organiza-tions throughout the U.S. As you read their interview, I believe you will see that they are the personification of passionately helpful entrepreneurs.

Tony & Mary Miller
The Dream Manager™

Tony and Mary Miller had a vision for Jancoa®, their Cincinnati-based janitorial service. They felt certain that if they could give their employees, the majority of whom are unskilled immigrants, the chance to dream about a bigger future, not only would their employees benefit, Jancoa™ would thrive and grow. To make their vision a reality, they created The Dream Manager™, a Unique Process that has made Jancoa the benchmark in its industry, and is now creating a buzz in related industries. Their story is as heart-warming as it is inspiring.

Dan Sullivan: Let's talk with you first, Tony, because I know you overcame a lot of challenges to get where you are today. How did it all get started?
Tony Miller: Well, Dan, when I was nineteen years old, my father went in for a triple bypass and he didn't make it out of the recovery room. That would be 1972. I remember as he was going into surgery, he told me just to focus on doing my very best in life, whatever that meant, and to always respect other people.

Dan Sullivan: Now as I understand it, Tony, you faced a lot of hurdles growing up in terms of your experience inside the education system. Would you mind talking about some of these issues?
Tony Miller: Sure, Dan. I think it's important for the readers to know where I came from, because it has a lot to do with where I am today and how I approach my business. Basically, for much of my childhood, I was unable to read. I'd moved to a bunch of different schools, and I had this secret. The secret was that I couldn't read. I remember saying to my father that he just needed to get used to the fact that I was dumb and stupid. One day my teacher came up and said in front of the entire class, "Oh, my! You can't read." She didn't do that to be mean. She was gen-

uinely surprised because, for all that time, she thought I wasn't doing well because I didn't try hard or was lazy, when in fact I couldn't read.

Dan Sullivan: *So she found you a tutor.*

Tony Miller: That's right. This tutor taught me that the most important thing anyone can do in life is simply "show up," regardless of their situation. And she rewarded me for showing up at her house. She always had Oreo cookies, and you got one if you showed up, one if you tried hard, and another one if you succeeded. What she was basically trying to teach me is that if you want to gain the fruits of the world, you need to show up and try. If you fail, you need to get up and try again. Not only did I learn to read, 28 years ago I overcame a major alcohol addiction, and of course I grew my business from scratch. So my life has really been a lesson in persistence.

Dan Sullivan: *That's a very powerful story, Tony. Thank you for sharing it with us. I met you in 1990, and you had already been in the business for 18 years. So why don't you talk a bit about those first 18 years?*

Tony Miller: Well, when my father died, I was going to school full-time at the University of Cincinnati, and I needed to make some extra money. I decided that cleaning would be a great business to go into. I worked very hard and didn't make any money for a long time, always went in early, never took vacations. I didn't really understand that I could own the business rather than having the business own me.

Dan Sullivan: *What kinds of jobs were you doing in those early days?*

Tony Miller: We did vinyl repair. We did pressure washing. We did carpet cleaning. We did one-day-a-week jobs. We did five-day-a-week jobs. We did nursing homes. We did bank branches.

We did Class-A office buildings. Basically, we did jobs that virtually everyone else didn't want because they were either too hard or didn't pay enough.

Dan Sullivan: *Now, if you look at that period, I'm sure there were some significant growth points along the way, because when I met you in 1990, you were obviously quite a substantial company.*
Tony Miller: In 1990, I think we had about 65 part-time employees. Then we started to delegate some of the work and hire some managers and training people. We upgraded our jobs and started specializing in certain kinds of jobs. These were important steps, because previously we had done everything for everyone.

Dan Sullivan: *And then you brought in your wife, Mary.*
Tony Miller: Exactly. And that was probably the best decision I ever made. She was working for a great company, but her immediate supervisor was very obnoxious. We thought it couldn't get any worse, so we decided to work together. I remember the first day she started, she wanted to go through the budgets of all the jobs. My favorite job at the time was a job cleaning bank branches that brought in $25,000 a month. Mary added up all the costs and found out that we were losing $10,000 a year on the job. I had worked on that job for ten years and didn't even realize we were losing money. So Mary was able to weed out all the unprofitable jobs and, fortunately, we still had a lot of profitable jobs to focus on.

Dan Sullivan: *But at this stage you were still working, what, 18-hour days?*
Tony Miller: On a good day, it was 18 hours. Seven days a week, 24 hours a day, we had somebody in the company who was working—even on Christmas. We had a phone in our home, and people would check in at all hours of the night. If somebody

didn't show up or a job needed to be covered, I would get in my car and drive to clean the building. The sad part is that I thought this was normal. I didn't even realize that there was a different way to operate.

Dan Sullivan: *Of course, you were supporting your family too, right?*
Tony Miller: Yes, that was a big part of it. Early on in his life, my brother developed Hodgkin's disease, which is a form of cancer. Before my dad died, he said to me, "If anything happens to me, you're responsible for the family." I promised him I would take responsibility, and I didn't want to let my dad down. So that was an extra burden.

Dan Sullivan: *Let's bring Mary into the conversation, because I know that she made an extraordinary contribution right from the beginning. Mary, describe your background before you started working with Tony.*
Mary Miller: Well, I was a commissioned salesperson for eight years in the insurance industry. Before that I worked ten years at a company called U.S. Shoe, so I actually had first-hand experience as a salaried employee. I saw at a very early age what happens when a corporation doesn't take care of its employees —the problems that can be caused by turnover and low morale. I was determined that if I ever had the opportunity to be a business owner, I would do things differently.

Dan Sullivan: *Of course you probably didn't anticipate that your business would be in the cleaning industry.*
Mary Miller: (Laughing) I guess I always thought I would be in the kind of business that operates with a standard 8 to 5 day, Monday through Friday, and here I married a guy who was running a 24/7 business.

Dan Sullivan: *He probably only wanted you to work half the time and didn't care which 12 hours a day, right?*

Mary Miller: Within my first month working with him, I worked my first 26-hour day. When I got home, Tony was sitting there smiling. I'm like, "What are you so happy about?" He said, "Christmas came early." Never before did Tony have someone with the same dedication to the business who was willing to do whatever it takes. So we were on the same page from the beginning.

Dan Sullivan: *I'm sure you each brought different strengths to the table and complemented each other really well.*

Mary Miller: Absolutely. Tony really understood how the buildings needed to be cleaned and how to make the customer happy. He was less comfortable doing a lot of big selling and managing the relationships with clients. Tony also had trouble developing systems to manage all the information. I mean, he didn't have any computers when I started with him. He told everybody that I was dragging him into the 21st century. Now, of course, everything is computerized.

Dan Sullivan: *Tony, I know you also brought a lot of strengths to the table. What are some of the personal qualities that you found most helpful in developing the business?*

Tony Miller: I think my best strengths are that I'm both persistent and a simplifier of things. During the period when I couldn't read, I developed memory tricks. I got in the habit of simplifying. You know, in the cleaning industry we have 20- to 30-page documents that specify how things are supposed to be done. And I was able to zero in on the three or four things that needed to be done in every building. When many of your cleaning employees can't read or speak the language, it's very helpful if you can focus them on those three or four key tasks.

Mary Miller: I want to interject here, Dan, because Tony really deserves more credit than he's usually willing to give himself. In 1995, we hired a consultant who was supposedly going to come in and help us with a bunch of issues. What we discovered really quickly was that Tony knew a heck of a lot more than this high-priced consultant. So that was a really important experience in terms of boosting Tony's confidence.

Dan Sullivan: *Let's shift gears a bit and talk about the Unique Processes that you've developed, because I know you've really brought a lot of innovation in to the cleaning industry.*

Tony Miller: Sure. We have three different processes that complement each other. The first Unique Process that really made a big difference was The Facility Optimizer Process™. Basically, the goal here is to clean the same amount of space with smaller teams in a shorter period of time. Our competitors were cleaning 3,500 square feet an hour per person, yet because we were paying more benefits, we had to clean between 5,500 and 6,500 square feet per hour. Many companies separate the employees and put them on different floors so they never have another person to talk to. We found that if you operate with smaller teams, but let everyone on the team stick together, the employees really work hard. We're paying about $2 an hour more than our competitors and the employees realize this, so it really motivates them to produce results.

Dan Sullivan: *That's great. Now what about your grout-cleaning process?*

Tony Miller: We developed this process to deal with a very specific challenge we were facing. Basically, our customers were saying to us, "You're doing a great job, but these restroom floors look horrible." We were spending an enormous amount of time working on the problem with very poor results. I remember sitting the team down and doing a Strategy Circle*. We asked ourselves, "What do we have to do to deliver the result our customers want—brand-new-looking floors." We eventually came up with a process to address this issue.

Dan Sullivan: The interesting thing here is that you took a problem that the industry wasn't solving. People would wash the floors down every night, but that didn't make the floors look any better. So you pioneered an entirely new process that not only cleaned the floors but actually restored them, is that correct?
Mary Miller: That's right, Dan. We started doing it in the evening, and customers would come in the next day wondering how we had replaced the restroom floor in one night.

Dan Sullivan: That became a huge competitive advantage, didn't it?
Tony Miller: You bet. People, even the largest competitor, would say they could recognize a building Jancoa cleaned because the restrooms and lobbies always looked great.

Dan Sullivan: As your reputation grew, what happened to your client size and the kinds of customers you had access to?
Tony Miller: As I said before, we started out doing everything. Now, we don't do any buildings less than 100,000 square feet. So there's quite a bit of difference between 3,000 square feet and 100,000 square feet.

Dan Sullivan: You're generally operating in the Cincinnati metropolitan area, right?
Tony Miller: Yes, the greater Cincinnati area, which includes parts of northern Kentucky.

Mary Miller: Let me add that some of the largest cleaning companies in the country are located here in Cincinnati. Yet during a recent study, we found that we have a 25 percent market share. The closest competitors are at 16 percent each. You know, many of these companies always considered us a kind of mom-and-pop operation. They were very nice to us when we saw them at industry events. Then they realized that we have a 25 percent market share, and they're not so friendly anymore.

Dan Sullivan: *These companies are probably also trying to keep up with your innovative labor policies. Why don't we talk about your human resource philosophy, because I know you've put a lot of energy into this area, and it's reflected in your third Unique Process, The Dream Manager.*

Mary Miller: We'd love to talk about that, Dan. First of all, most janitorial companies don't have many full-time employees. We've made a strong commitment to making more of our janitorial workforce full time. But The Dream Manager process is all about how we treat these employees once they start working for us. Our basic message to employees is that no matter where you come from, no matter what level of income or education you've attained, you can lead a productive, fulfilling life, and you can make your dreams become reality.

Dan Sullivan: *Where are your employees normally coming from?*

Tony Miller: Well, we have a lot of lower-skilled immigrant workers who come from all over the world—Latin America, Europe, Africa. Somehow, they end up in Cincinnati, and they learn through the immigrant networks that Jancoa is a great place to work, with great pay and benefits. They know that this is a place where they can come and get started, learn some tools, and hopefully move on to bigger things.

Dan Sullivan: *Could you describe some of the specific benefits that are so attractive to employees?*

Mary Miller: First of all, our wages are generally higher than any of our competitors, and, again, we've made a commitment to bringing people in at a full-time level. Once we hire employees, we put them through a paid training program before they ever set foot on a job. Some of the other benefits are really quite innovative in the industry. For example, because many of our workers are coming from Third World countries, we provide TB testing. If a worker tests positive, then we work closely with the health department to get them the appropriate care. And to make sure they can afford whatever care they need, regardless of the health issue, we offer medical insurance. We also offer paid vacation time, which can increase in length the longer an employee stays with us.

Dan Sullivan: *Let me stop you there, Mary, because the vacation time you're offering really seems remarkable by industry standards. You know how much I've emphasized to all my clients in Strategic Coach the importance of free time. And I bet it's an extraordinary experience for these employees, who are probably used to working non-stop, to take some quality free time for themselves and their families. Could you talk a little more about how this policy came about?*

Mary Miller: Well, you certainly were influential in getting us to move in this direction. The free time was something we talked about for a long time, and finally we just took action and implemented the policy. You know, for the first couple of years, many employees were not taking advantage of it because they didn't understand the concept of "no work, still get paid." They thought that no work meant no money. In most countries of the world, holidays are a foreign concept. But once our employees started realizing that they could take this time off without being penalized, they really started taking advantage of it.

Dan Sullivan: *I'm sure that when people are new to a country, don't speak the language, and may be working two or three jobs to support their family, the extra free time is just invaluable.*

Mary Miller: Absolutely. I mean it certainly gives people an opportunity to get to know their community better. It certainly

> *The typical turnover in the cleaning industry is around 350 percent per year ... Tony and I started looking at each other and saying, "How do we stop the revolving door? How do we create an environment that will attract the best people?" So that's how The Dream Manager came about.*

gives them some extra time to take care of administrative matters like getting their kids into school and applying for the appropriate licenses. We've also discovered that it gives people an opportunity to go back home and see the family they've left behind. They can leave for an extended period without having to quit their job, which is really unusual in most cases.

Tony Miller: Let me add that even our key managers only work four-day weeks. I'm sure we're the only contractor in the world that has its general managers and supervisors only working four days a week. What that means is that they have to learn how to hand the baton over to somebody else. They have an incentive to learn additional skills, because they don't want to be calling another manager on his day off for instructions on how to do something. Our people love this extra day off, and it really allows them to come in motivated to do a really great job.

Dan Sullivan: I'm sure turnover has always been a big problem in the janitorial industry. And what's striking to me as I listen to this is that you've basically created a human resource system that dramatically improves employee retention.

Mary Miller: That's correct. The typical turnover in the cleaning industry is around 350 percent per year. There were months in our business where we'd hire 50 or 60 people and go through all of them. At one time, we were 38 full-time people short. Tony and I started looking at each other and saying, "How do we stop the revolving door? How do we create an environment that will attract the best people?" So that's how The Dream Manager came about.

Dan Sullivan: *How many employees do you have now?*
Tony Miller: We have 300 full-time employees, so we're the largest janitorial company in Cincinnati. And we really have a great pipeline, because 87 percent of our new employees were recruited or recommended by current employees.

Dan Sullivan: *That's fantastic. And not only are you attracting and retaining employees, you're also putting them in the best position to be efficient and productive.*
Tony Miller: Exactly. That gets back to the tools and systems associated with our processes. One of the things we've done when we're dealing with a one-million-square-foot building is help our employees focus on the three most important things that need to be accomplished in that building. What's at the top of the client's priority list? Usually, it's the lobby areas, the restrooms, and the executive areas. We started focusing all our attention on making sure the client never has a problem with our work in any of these high-value areas. By simplifying things, we make huge buildings a lot more manageable to our employees.

Dan Sullivan: *Could you share some specific examples of the kinds of experiences you've had by operating through these processes?*
Mary Miller: Sure. We had one employee who was with a competitor for over 15 years—one of the largest in the country. We took over the building she was working on and retained her as manager. At first she was very skeptical, but within the first 30 days, she was totally blown away by the ways our systems made her job so much easier. The building had never been cleaner.

Dan Sullivan: *A great credit to your systems. I understand that some very large corporations across the country want to partner with you on your cleaning process?*

Tony Miller: That's right. We have a huge company we're working with that cleans restaurants across the country. They were under the impression that you actually have to rip out floors to get the results we're getting in restrooms. You'd be losing $10,000 a year every time you did that. So they really believe that our process is the key to successful bathroom cleaning.

Dan Sullivan: *How do you approach sales situations?*

Tony Miller: That's an interesting question, Dan, because a lot of our work comes outside of the bidding process, which is unusual in this industry. Basically, a lot of our business comes through word of mouth. Somebody's in a building and says, "Boy, your bathrooms look great. Who does your work here?" Next thing you know, we get a call from a new prospect wanting to know if we can clean their buildings. So we sit down and negotiate and determine on a case-by-case basis what kind of price is appropriate based on the client's needs.

Dan Sullivan: *You've totally escaped from the downward pressure on prices created by the bid model.*

Tony Miller: It's been incredibly empowering. Whereas our competitors may lose customers every month because of price or quality issues, we keep our customers and continue adding new customers. And we've also been able to turn down business. We had a $25,000-a-month customer who didn't treat our employees right, so we had to fire him. Our message was, "We can't deal with someone who does not understand that people are our greatest asset. You don't understand how to treat people, so we can't do business with you."

Dan Sullivan: *What I see, Tony, and this gets back to The Dream*

Manager, is a real human connection. Given your life experiences, you probably have a tremendous amount of empathy for people who can't read or write and are struggling in the world.

Tony Miller: I've cried when employees come in, because I can tell immediately that they can't read or write and don't want anybody to know. What I've always wanted to do is create a safe place for them to come in and do their best, without worrying about whether they look right or talk right. You know, many of our best managers have been people with a seventh- or eighth-grade education. They're always worried about misspelling words and things like that. I can write something down on a piece of paper, and they look at it and laugh, because they see that I'm not really any smarter than they are. So there's a huge bond being able to share that experience.

Dan Sullivan: *That's just phenomenal.*

Tony Miller: Thanks, Dan. You know, my tutor's name was Mrs. Lumley, and we try to be just as inviting as Mrs. Lumley was to me. Her philosophy was that if you just show up, good things will start to happen for you. That's what The Dream Manager is all about: giving people a safe environment where they can feel comfortable coming to work. We know that if they just have the confidence to show up, opportunities will start to open for them.

Dan Sullivan: *And plenty of Oreo cookies.*

Tony Miller: (Laughing) Exactly. Lots of Oreos.

Dan Sullivan: *Do you have any thoughts on this, Mary?*

Mary Miller: I think one thing we should emphasize is that despite our focus on retaining employees, we are really excited about giving people the chance to "outgrow us" and move on to other opportunities. That's what The Dream Manager is designed for—giving people new skills and helping them achieve personal growth. We're actually working with our janitorial clients to see

That's what The Dream Manager is all about: giving people a safe environment where they can feel comfortable coming to work. We know that if they just have the confidence to show up, opportunities will start to open for them.

where there might be new opportunities for employees. You know, these clients interact with our cleaners on a daily basis and have first-hand awareness of their incredible professionalism. Many clients are quite eager to hire some of our best employees away from us by giving them maintenance positions or things of that nature. And we encourage employees to go and realize those opportunities.

Dan Sullivan: *That must send an incredibly strong message to your employee base.*
Mary Miller: It's been really powerful. People are excited that tomorrow can be different and better than today. When they see that their employer really cares about making their dreams a reality, they become very productive and very loyal.

Dan Sullivan: *Could you talk a little about your home ownership program, because it's really quite remarkable?*
Mary Miller: Sure. We partnered with a non-profit here in Cincinnati. The goal is to put our employees through a training process that helps them understand everything involved with buying a home. We've helped about 18 families purchase their own home, and almost every one of them was a first generation homeowner. One woman, Gloria, is an incredible woman who's a supervisor for our company. She worried every night toward the last hour of her work shift about whether she was going to get home safely, because there was a dark hallway in her apartment that the drug dealers essentially controlled. Once she got her

own home, not only did she lose the worry, she became much more productive on the job. She was able to focus attention on helping other employees who had needs.

Dan Sullivan: *That's a great story.*
Mary Miller: It is. Gloria's a fifty-five-year-old African American woman, and nobody in her family has ever owned a home. So this had a profound impact on her daughter and her grand-daughter. One day, the principal of the school that her grand-daughter attends called us and said, "Could you come talk to our parents about this program? We can't get our students to dream, because the parents have stopped dreaming." So the home-owner program is sort of a gift that keeps on giving.

Dan Sullivan: *You also offer English classes, right?*
Mary Miller: Absolutely. We have English classes. We provide access to a lot of ESL classes throughout the city, but because our employees work different hours, many of them can't make these classes. So we've created our own. You know, the focus of our program is just to provide an environment where people can keep dreaming. Whether the goal is to improve their finances, get a GED certificate or college degree, improve their personal habits, help family members in other countries, or mend relation-ships, we help people set goals and plan for their future.

Dan Sullivan: *I'm sure you've got a ton of inspirational stories. Are there any others you want to share with us?*
Mary Miller: One of my favorites involves a holiday party our company held that brought everybody together. We had employees make Dream Boards, where they cut words and pictures out of magazines and glued them on these black foam boards to represent their dreams for the future. Now we had a lot of Hispanics in attendance, who typically tell us, "No com-prende. No speak English." Tony and I went around the room

and asked people, "Tell me what these pictures mean. What are your dreams?" Every single person was able to converse with us and talk about their dreams. Not a single person said they didn't understand what we were asking.

Dan Sullivan: *That's such a great story, and I'm sure you have many others.*

Mary Miller: We had one couple, Freddie and Marie. They met through our company, and they were the first Hispanic couple to buy a home through our home ownership program. Now they actually own their own cleaning business. We gave them some seed money and started them up with a customer so they could take this leap.

Dan Sullivan: *You know, the issue of immigration has become such a hot topic in the U.S. The whole process of helping immigrants become productive citizens is such an important national project. And what's striking to me, Mary and Tony, is that I think you've come up with one of the best models out there for addressing this issue in a positive way.*

Mary Miller: Thank you, Dan. That means a lot.

Dan Sullivan: *It also occurs to me that all of your processes are very scalable. Jancoa may only be in Cincinnati, but you can teach them across the United States.*

Mary Miller: We're definitely working on packaging our processes. We're developing some licensing programs, and national companies are expressing interest. We're also working with a best-selling author to produce a book on The Dream Manager that will be out soon. So things are really progressing.

Dan Sullivan: *Tony, you've gone from being someone who for much of your childhood was basically illiterate, you battled alcoholism three decades ago, and in the early days of your business*

We envision a time when every company, every school, and every church can use The Dream Manager to give people hope and opportunity no matter where they are.

spent all of your time working, to now to being a real intellectual capital developer. Let's look down the road ten years. You've got three very powerful pieces of intellectual capital. What are you looking to achieve ten years down the road?

Tony Miller: For The Dream Manager, it's simple. We envision a time when every company, every school, and every church can use The Dream Manager to give people hope and opportunity no matter where they are. We'd also like to see our restroom program used across the country so that any bathroom is as clean as it can be. And we hope to get contractors across the country certified and licensed to use The Facility Optimizer Process.

Mary Miller: If I could sum up what Tony just said, we ultimately want Jancoa to become like the Good Housekeeping Seal for cleaning, where you can tell just by looking at the building that a Jancoa process has been used.

Dan Sullivan: That's fantastic. What a great story.
Mary Miller: Thank you, Dan, for helping us write it.

For contact details on The Dream Manager, please see page 214.

Differentiation

Differentiation

All entrepreneurs in every marketplace need to differentiate themselves in positive and appealing ways in the eyes of existing and potential clientele. Some entrepreneurs are obviously better at doing this than others. For example, Richard Rossi and his partner, Barbara Harris, at Envision EMI have positioned themselves uniquely in the minds of the best teachers, the brightest students, and the most committed parents around the world.

The problem in their marketplace is not a lack of educational offerings for grade school and high school students; the problem is linking up the best and brightest students with the unique learning opportunities and experiences that make their highly dedicated parents and teachers excited about the students' future prospects.

Richard and Barbara have solved this problem in a way that differentiates Envision EMI from all other organizations.

Tony and Mary Miller have cornered the market on attracting highly motivated and loyal immigrant employees to their janitorial company—and have attracted the best customers because they are able to provide the best cleaning teams in the industry. The problem in their industry is not a lack of people to hire; the problem is how to attract, train, and keep the best workers to provide highly satisfactory results every night, year after year. Tony and Mary have differentiated themselves because they have solved this problem to their customers' satisfaction, and their competitors haven't.

Having a better understanding of what clients want.
Much of the skill that makes one entrepreneurial company better than others lies in having a clearer, deeper understanding of what prospective and existing clients are looking for. The value of products and services is never inherent. In fact, they have no value whatsoever if customers don't want to pay for them. Even more significant is the realization that, deep down, consumers aren't looking for products or services at all.

Gary Boomer and his team understand that accounting firms are not looking for new computer technology. The problem isn't a lack of technology; the problem is a lack of understanding of how to maximize the usefulness of technology.

What these firms are looking for are fundamental strategies and processes that enable them to be more productive and profitable using their existing capabilities and resources. Gary has differentiated his consulting firm by combining his knowledge of accountants with an understanding of how technology makes accounting firms better.

Making life more enjoyable, rewarding, and exciting.
All consumers in all markets are continually looking for breakthrough solutions that will make their present situations more rewarding and enjoyable, and their future situations more exciting and certain. David Allen and his team at The Allen Groupe understand that owners, pilots, and mechanics in the private jet industry aren't interested in cleaning and detailing. In fact, they don't want to think about it at all. They just want the problem to go away, permanently. David and his group handle this in such a unique and satisfying fashion that private jet airports around the world are clamoring for their process. All of the entrepreneurs featured in this book have a great

understanding of what their clients are trying to achieve in their lives. Products and services are not the issue here. Ambition, satisfaction, and fulfillment are. Because Unique Process entrepreneurs understand this, they continually create and provide solutions that differentiate them from everyone else in their industries.

Why the "problem" is never really the problem.
The vast majority of entrepreneurs in all markets organize their lives around the marketing and selling of commodities. These are in the form of products and services that are designed to solve specific problems and deliver specific benefits. Our world today is filled with countless numbers of these commoditized solutions, most of which fail to deliver satisfaction because the companies delivering them don't understand what the real problem is. Joe Polish understands that homeowners are not looking for great carpet cleaning. It's not high on their list of desirable lifetime goals and experiences. What they are looking for is peace of mind before, and satisfaction after, the unpleasant, unavoidable, periodic disruption of having workers come into the privacy of their homes to do the cleaning.

What all of these examples point out is that, from a consumer's perspective, the problem is never the problem. The problem isn't the lack of educational services, janitorial workers, computer technology, or carpet cleaners. *The problem is how to think about all of these things, make decisions, and take effective actions in a way that increases consumers' sense of enjoyment, satisfaction, and excitement about their present and future lives.*

Wiser, more fundamental, more lasting solutions.
Commoditized products and services never solve this kind of problem. On the other hand, Unique Processes of the kind represented by our featured entrepreneurs always do so, in

ways that differentiate them in a positive, appealing, impactful, and permanent fashion. Over time, their continual delivery of wiser, more fundamental, more comprehensive, more lasting solutions in the marketplace differentiates them from everyone else. It also automatically makes them into Industry Transformers.

John Ferrell is a member of the legal industry, which is often accused of being more interested in increasing billable hours than in providing useful solutions. From reading his interview, I think you'll agree that John is a total exception to the stereotypes. You'll see that he is one of the most passionately useful lawyers you could encounter. John didn't start off as a lawyer. As an electrical engineer, he first came into contact with high-tech entrepreneurs who were trying to start new businesses based on their innovations and inventions. Even before he got his law degree, John understood that there was a fundamental problem that most startup entrepreneurs weren't solving, and neither were the lawyers who were advising them. This was the marketplace opportunity that enabled John to differentiate himself.

John Ferrell
Strategic IP Process

In the midst of the dot-com bust in 2002, John Ferrell, a successful patent attorney in Palo Alto, realized that he was swiftly becoming commoditized. He also had a pivotal breakthrough in thinking: He discovered the most important thing that businesses should be protecting — and it wasn't their products and services. The result was Strategic IP, the Unique Process that John created to turn his newfound wisdom into unlimited opportunity and to free himself from commoditization forever.

Dan Sullivan: It's a real pleasure to talk with John Ferrell, who I believe is one of the most exciting lawyers in the United States right now. Through his Strategic IP Process, John is totally redefining what it means to be an intellectual property attorney, or any attorney for that matter. Let's begin, John, with some biographical information, because I know you have an interesting background.

John Ferrell: Sure, Dan. I grew up in Texas and eventually studied engineering in graduate school — chemical and electrical engineering. After graduate school I became a practicing engineer for a few years, but I wasn't a very good engineer. I just didn't have the attention span necessary to work on projects that could last for years. So I went back to school to become a patent attorney.

Dan Sullivan: What attracted you to patent law?
John Ferrell: I just fell in love with the whole process of protecting technology and learning about new inventions.

Dan Sullivan: So you went to work for a large firm.
John Ferrell: Yes. I was an associate at a large law firm writing patent applications for big companies, but I didn't find

that process particularly satisfying because there were just so many patents and so many attorneys involved. And individual patents really didn't seem to have much value to the big companies I was representing. Then, in 1992, I started my own law firm with a couple of friends, and we primarily focused on serving entrepreneurs.

Dan Sullivan: *But you were still essentially a patent attorney.*
John Ferrell: Yes. I still described myself as a patent attorney. When clients came in, the focus was always "what have you invented, what's new about your invention, and how can we protect it?" Throughout the 1990s, I actually became fairly successful as a patent writer. I was named one of the top rainmakers in the state of California based on number of billings. So we built up a very nice practice in Silicon Valley, with wonderful clients. But our business was still primarily focused on preparing and filing patent applications, and counseling people on patent issues.

Dan Sullivan: *And then the dot-com bust hit Silicon Valley.*
John Ferrell: In 2002, in the midst of the dot-com bust, a lot of internet companies went out of business, and so, of course, this impacted all the law firms that were serving these companies. About 20 of our competitors went bankrupt and closed their doors. The largest law firm in California was located in the building right across the parking lot from us. They had 900 attorneys, and in January of 2003, they went bankrupt. So that just gives you a sense of what was happening in California, where thousands and thousands of lawyers were being laid off.

Dan Sullivan: *How many attorneys did your firm have at the time?*
John Ferrell: Forty attorneys and around 50 staff.

Dan Sullivan: *Were you forced to lay anybody off?*
John Ferrell: We did lay off five attorneys, which was difficult. But we managed to survive the downturn through the incredible fiscal responsibility of my remaining co-founding partner. We did not have any debt. But it was still scary, because our billings really took a nosedive.

Dan Sullivan: *Now, in the heat of this downturn, something started happening to the patent business. Could you talk a little about what transpired?*
John Ferrell: Well, it's quite simple really. For a span of almost ten years, we were charging $15,000 for a patent application. That was just the going rate. And then around the time of the dot-com bust, patent applications started being outsourced to India. There were technical writers over there who were turning out patent applications for $1,500, one-tenth of our cost. IBM shifted much of its patent-drafting team to Bangalore, India, and other companies followed suit.

Dan Sullivan: *That's a really good example of commoditization.*
John Ferrell: Exactly. We discovered, much to our surprise and disbelief, that we had become commoditized. We weren't really selling legal services and legal expertise. We were selling $15,000 patents that were now worth $1,500.

> We discovered, much to our surprise and disbelief, that we had become commoditized. We weren't really selling legal services and legal expertise. We were selling $15,000 patents that were now worth $1,500.

Dan Sullivan: *John, that was about the time you came into the Strategic Coach Program, wasn't it?*

John Ferrell: January 2003 was really the peak in terms of our competitors going out of business, and I came into the Coach program in February 2003. So it was really excellent timing, because the Coach helped me think seriously about what it means to become commoditized, and how to escape that predicament. I remember so clearly the plane ride back from Chicago after my first workshop, thinking, "Here I am in a class with a lot of highly successful entrepreneurs who are growing their businesses, and I'm just struggling to stay profitable in the current environment." So I just faced up to the commoditization and really decided that "enough is enough."

Dan Sullivan: *You started moving away from this dependence on $15,000 patent applications.*

John Ferrell: Yes. I started to realize that clients really don't care about patents. What they want is control over their market space, and patents are only a means to an end. Every business provides some sort of unique experience to their customers. It's just a question of defining what that experience is, and figuring out how to monopolize it. Because if you have monopolized the experience, you can monopolize the customer. Competition becomes irrelevant. So I totally realigned my legal practice to focus on how patents and other intellec-

The question for companies is: What are you trying to protect? It's not the invention. It's not the technology. It's the customer relationship and the unique experience that brings customers back.

tual property tools can help companies achieve the experience monopoly they desire.

Dan Sullivan: *John, I know you've developed a really powerful Unique Process, Strategic IP , to help companies deal with these issues. So why don't you walk us through the different dimensions of the process, because it's all very innovative.*

John Ferrell: Sure. One of the advantages of working with startup companies in Silicon Valley is that I've observed hundreds and hundreds of cases where a company either dies and goes bankrupt, or succeeds and is acquired, in a relatively short period of time. Over the years, I've identified five strategies that really successful companies seem to follow. So we've made these strategies the basis of our Strategic IP program.

Dan Sullivan: *I'm intrigued. Let's hear the first strategy.*

John Ferrell: The first strategy involves "content." The question for companies is: What are you trying to protect? It's not the invention. It's not the technology. It's the customer relationship and the unique experience that brings customers back. I always tell clients that if you lose your way and become confused about what's important in your business, go to the very first page of your company website. Because nearly every company, on the first page of its website, has a list of reasons why customers should be there. Often they're listed in bullet points—or what I call "silver bullets." These are the experiences we want to protect and monopolize. So that's The Silver Bullet Strategy.

Dan Sullivan: *Great. And next?*

John Ferrell: The second strategy involves "architecture." In other words, how do you build an architecture that efficiently protects your marketplace experience? What we've discovered is that the best way to protect an experience is by strategically clustering groups of intellectual property—copyrights, trademarks, patents, licensing agreements. When multiple clusters overlap, they reinforce each other and really provide a strong layer of protection. We then have the ability to graphically illustrate for our clients how different clusters of intellectual property relate, while creating a "cluster map" that describes the pathway we are going to follow to provide maximum protection. That's The Architecture Strategy or Cluster Strategy.

Dan Sullivan: *Right. And third?*

John Ferrell: The third strategy, while a bit complicated, is a critical component of Strategic IP. Basically, one of the big problems that companies have with respect to patents is that they are afraid competitors are going to design around their inventions. The patents are no longer valuable because a competitor has simply found another way to do things. I have several responses to this concern. First, if all you are doing is protecting a technology or protecting an invention, then, of course, somebody can find a way to do things better and get around your patent. But if you find a way to protect your customer experience, then when a competitor comes along, they will always end up delivering a different experience. So your competitors won't be able to replicate that experience.

Dan Sullivan: *It's all about the unique experience.*

John Ferrell: That's right, Dan. The second part of the answer gets to what I call The Continuity Strategy. The crux of The Continuity Strategy is that before an important patent application issues into a patent, a continuation application is filed with the patent office, which keeps alive the original filing and the important filing date. These continuation applications can be used to prevent minor "design-arounds." If a competitor changes their product slightly to avoid an issued patent, we have a back-up patent that can often be modified to cover the new design.

Dan Sullivan: *Like a "gotcha."*
John Ferrell: Absolutely. I've had this trick pulled on me several times in my career, with a few bloody noses to show for it. You learn from your scars.

Dan Sullivan: *What strikes me, John, is that this intellectual property game has both an offensive and a defensive aspect. You need to operate on both ends of the field. So could you talk a little about this dimension?*
John Ferrell: That's a great observation, Dan, and it gets to the fourth strategy of our process, which is all about "defense." Now, you may be wondering, "What exactly do these companies have to defend against?" And I'll tell you that the biggest legal threat facing all of our clients is the prospect of patent litigation. Not every entrepreneur gets sued, but every successful entrepreneur faces the threat of litigation. And when it happens, it can be devastating because it is so distracting. It can really negatively affect a good startup. So I have come up with some pretty simple methods for inoculating a company against patent litigation. One approach I call The Porcupine Quill Strategy. The basic focus is to build a coat of pointed intellectual property protections, or quills, around a company so that if a competitor tries to sue, they are going to be stabbed by any number of these porcupine quills and hence be deterred from attacking.

Dan Sullivan: *So that's essentially a defensive strategy.*
John Ferrell: Yes. And once we have a strong defense in place,

You know, intellectual property isn't a technology tool; it's a marketing tool. It's about opening up some market space for your sales guys.

we can move on to a more offensive strategy, which represents the fifth stage of our Strategic IP Process. The focus is using a company's intellectual property portfolio in an aggressive way to actually take market share away from competitors. What this amounts to is acquiring an understanding of who the competitors are, and where they are going with respect to product development, so we can then design our intellectual property holdings to cover their product road map. It is an incredibly strong strategy when you're in a tough competitive environment.

Dan Sullivan: I was completely ignorant of this area of expertise before I met you, John. And what I find so remarkable from an entrepreneurial standpoint is that you've found a way to use the law for both product development on the one hand, and marketing on the other.

John Ferrell: I certainly see it that way, and this approach has opened up a world of possibilities for what the law can be. You know, intellectual property is not a technology tool; it is a marketing tool. It is about opening up some market space for your sales guys.

Dan Sullivan: And securing it.

John Ferrell: Securing it—that is exactly right. Most lawyers are not really trained to generate sales. It is not part of their legal training to go out and help marketing departments succeed. I'm blessed to be in a position where my legal experience can be used to help companies successfully improve their marketplace position.

Dan Sullivan: But you're also contributing to product design— product in the "experience" sense of the word.

John Ferrell: That's right. One of the stories I like to tell involves the ski equipment industry. In the early 1990s, a new kind of parabolic or hourglass-shaped ski was introduced that could substitute for the more traditional straight skis. The result was a total industry transformation. These new hourglass-shaped skis made it possible for casual skiers to go out three or four weekends a year and enjoy skiing at a much higher skill level than they could with the older, more cumbersome skis. But the problem with these skis was that when you went downhill, they vibrated in a way that created resonance in the skis. The resonance was pretty minor, but it still caused tremendous leg fatigue. Then a sports company called K2 came along and invented a solution. They put piezoelectric crystals into the ski. Without getting into the technical aspects of how these crystals worked, and it really was quite amazing, the point is the crystals stabilized the skis by dampening them. But what's interesting is that the company got so focused on the technology, the piezoelectric crystal, that they seemed to lose sight of the big picture.

Dan Sullivan: *They lost sight of the experience.*
John Ferrell: Exactly. It wasn't the piezoelectric crystal that was important. It was the experience created by a dampened, more comfortable ski. So, of course, a number of other ski equipment companies came up with their own solution for dampening the vibrating ski. But had K2 focused on protecting the experience rather than the technology, it seems to me they could have totally owned that market space.

Dan Sullivan: *How would you have proceeded differently from an intellectual property perspective?*
John Ferrell: Basically, I would have encouraged K2 to think about protecting the improved ski experience, not just the widget that fixed the problem. By creating an intellectual prop-erty cluster around the reduced vibration, including patents on frequency shifting, dampening, filtering, and the like, K2 could have largely eliminated their competition. The idea is that you want to completely monopolize the experience of more comfort-

able skis. You want to have patents on all the important equipment elements that contribute to that experience.

Dan Sullivan: John, I know that you are bound by the etiquette of attorney-client privilege in terms of keeping a lot of your work confidential. But are there any stories that you'd feel comfortable sharing with us in regard to the outstanding work you've done on behalf of specific clients?

John Ferrell: Well, a story that I often tell involves a former client of mine, a company called Polycom, that designed the triangular speakerphone. Nearly two decades ago, founders Brian Hinman and Jeff Rodman came up with an idea for a conference room phone. They were hoping to raise venture money, and I helped them file four or five patents that covered the technology in their new phone. The phones sold very well, and the founders quickly discovered that there were two things people really liked about their product. The first was the phone's shape, something about the soft triangular contours made the phone seem to float on the conference table. The second was the rich, deep sound of the phone. It filled the conference room and created a big sound experience. So when Polycom started realizing that it was these experiences that sold the phones, they began to modify and change the phone design to reinforce these experiences. They developed a subwoofer that goes underneath the table to reinforce the big sound. They sold "spider" microphones that extend across the table to separate the speaker from the microphone, allowing greater speaker volume. And they developed hundreds of other tiny inventions and improvements that were protected through patents.

Dan Sullivan: So they essentially created an experience monopoly on the conference room speakerphone business.
John Ferrell: Exactly. Last time I checked, their market dominance was around 90 percent for their business conference room

space. Basically, for as long as my career lasts, you won't see another conference room phone manufacturer who can succeed without, in some way, going through the Polycom portfolio.

Dan Sullivan: *That's just remarkable. It really demonstrates what's possible when you use intellectual property law aggressively and creatively. Now that we've got a sense of your strategies, could you talk a little more about how the Strategic IP Process actually is structured from the time you start interacting with clients. How long does it usually take for clients to be up and running?*

John Ferrell: Well, I like to think of the process as a three-year process. In year one, we focus on "building," identifying the key experiences to be protected and laying the foundation for an eventual monopoly. In year two, we focus on "defending," looking at competitors from a defensive point of view. If we are going to get sued, who is going to sue us, and what are we going to do about it? Almost all of my super-successful clients run into some kind of IP legal attack from a competitor right about the time they are either being acquired or going public. It's very frustrating because unless there is a strategy in place to deal with this, it can greatly affect the value of the company.

Dan Sullivan: *Wow.*

John Ferrell: If we can identify problems ahead of time, there's a much better chance for a good outcome. Finally, the third year is a "competing" year. If my client's strategy is to exit through an acquisition, we'll identify potential acquisition candidates and try to understand how we can make our company most valuable to that acquirer. One way of doing this is to actually map our intellectual property around the target company's customer experience. The goal is to make the client essential to the target company, so that they actually have to acquire the client in order to operate effectively. So that's one indication of the kind of work we do.

Dan Sullivan: *It's almost a packaging exercise, isn't it?*
John Ferrell: Definitely.

Dan Sullivan: *And also from the standpoint of investors, your work must be tremendously reassuring.*
John Ferrell: Totally. Especially if you can look at competitors and say that over the last two years, we have been repositioning our intellectual property assets to dominate a particular market space.

Dan Sullivan: *Sometimes you actually take a position in a startup, don't you?*
John Ferrell: I used to take a position in nearly every startup I was involved in. It was part of my business model. I don't do that quite as much anymore, but I'll still frequently buy in and invest along with the A-round investors on venture-backed, early-stage clients. So investments certainly remain part of our strategy.

Dan Sullivan: *John, could you talk in broad terms about the scope of your client base? How many companies are you working with?*
John Ferrell: I think at this time we have over 200 companies. It's a pretty large number, though not all of the companies are to the point where they require a lot of attention.

Dan Sullivan: *Are you still working primarily with startups?*
John Ferrell: We certainly do work with a lot of startups and other technology-oriented companies in the Silicon Valley area. However, we also have clients around the world involved in virtually every business sector you can imagine. We are involved with some really exciting companies, such as the social networking company, Facebook.com, and Sony PlayStation, to name a couple.

Dan Sullivan: *What kind of compensation structure do you employ?*

John Ferrell: Well, I have really tried to get away from the hourly billing model, because I do not think it is good for clients, and it is certainly not good for lawyers. When you bill by the hour, there's no real incentive to deliver and produce results in an efficient way. So I have tried to shift as much work as possible over to flat fee billing, and I think clients are happier. But in terms of the legal profession as a whole, it will probably be a long time before we see a switch.

Dan Sullivan: *How is your firm structured, John? I mean, there are several different areas of focus, right?*

John Ferrell: That's right, Dan. We have three practice groups: corporate, litigation, and intellectual property. Although our IP practice comprises about half the firm, we offer a multi-disciplinary approach to working with clients, seamlessly collaborating across practice areas to provide quality service on a broad range of legal issues.

Dan Sullivan: *And you also handle all of the patents that come out of the process.*

John Ferrell: That is right. We still do the commodity piece, although it's no longer a commodity. It's an important strategic piece that allows us to implement the overall process.

Dan Sullivan: *What is the attitude toward Strategic IP from other members of your firm? Are there any skeptics?*

John Ferrell: Well, I would just say at a broad level that lawyers are very conservative by nature. Talking about monopolies in the way I talk about them can make some lawyers very nervous.

Dan Sullivan: *Almost like talking dirty, isn't it?*

John Ferrell: Exactly. From law school on, lawyers are trained to

Before, I was only selling two things: expertise and price. And that's a very difficult road to take in any industry. Now we have a powerful process that's not about preparing and filing patents. It's about helping our clients understand and monopolize their market space.

think that monopolies are bad, monopolies are evil, and monopolies will hurt you. But, of course, the kind of monopoly I am promoting does not involve collusion among large corporations or market manipulators.

Dan Sullivan: *It's an experience monopoly.*
John Ferrell: That is exactly right. All we are talking about here is monopolizing your customer base and allowing entrepreneurs to create an air supply that they can draw on while they get going.

Dan Sullivan: *This is especially important for startups because they can get wiped out so fast.*
John Ferrell: Absolutely. It is very difficult for entrepreneurs to get traction in any business. And, you know, almost every successful company in history has had some very significant marketplace advantage.

Dan Sullivan: *What about expansion? Do you see The Strategic IP Process moving beyond your firm, and do you see your firm expanding as a result of the process?*
John Ferrell: Well, we are growing. The difficulty is hiring good people, and we're continuing to do that. It's interesting, though, because we have two main sources of new business. The first is the venture capital community. Investors send their

clients over to get protection. The second largest source of referrals is other law firms. It really makes me feel good that colleagues in other law firms would send their clients over. I'm appreciative of that.

Dan Sullivan: *Have any other law firms become interested in doing what you're doing?*
John Ferrell: You know, colleagues call and invite me to lunch. They want to know how it is that my clients pay in advance each quarter for representation—they don't understand how that works. I just had lunch this past week with a friend who is with one of the really large national law firms. He was just amazed that we're able to make money at this patent business since so much of his firm's work has gone overseas or to smaller shops. I was at a trade show last summer, and the managing lawyer of a competing firm came up to me and said, "John, I'm not going to tell you where I got it, but I got hold of one of your books. I was going through trying to figure out what it says, but it's just full of 'Ferrell-speak.' I can't understand any of it."

Dan Sullivan: *Great. So you've done a really good job of monopolizing your own market space in the legal industry.*
John Ferrell: We're making progress, that's for sure.

Dan Sullivan: *John, let's just do a before-and-after: How did you think about things before you created The Strategic IP Process, and how do you look at things now?*
John Ferrell: Before, I was only selling two things: expertise and price. And that's a very difficult road to take in any industry. Now we have a powerful process that's not about preparing and filing patents. It is about helping our clients understand and monopolize their market space. When it comes to intellectual property law, we've left all our compet-

■ *I totally love what I'm doing, and I cannot wait to get into the office every morning. I mean that sincerely — it's just a wonderful way to spend my career.* ■

itors behind. We no longer have competitors. And I really do not have to worry about Bangalore, India, taking away my business. That is very important.

Dan Sullivan: You're a pretty long way from your days as a diesel mechanic in southern Texas.
John Ferrell: (Laughing) You know, growing up in southern Texas, I studied mechanics in high school. I was really interested in diesel engines and auto mechanics. If I wasn't going to be a tractor repairman, I actually thought seriously about opening up an auto repair shop in my small town. And then, of course, I eventually studied engineering before moving on to law.

Dan Sullivan: I just wanted to reflect on that because you've had a series of life experiences and developed certain kinds of specialties that are probably very unusual for people going into law. And I'd bet that your familiarization with engineering and technology early in life really helped you become such an effective intellectual property lawyer.
John Ferrell: I just love getting my hands dirty and solving problems. That's what intrigues me about technology—and about business. And I understand how hard it is to run a business. My grandfather was an immigrant who worked as a coal miner in a small New Mexico town. Business is tough. Small business is even tougher, and I love being part of it.

Dan Sullivan: *John, it's been a pleasure talking with you. You're such a free thinker about so many things.*
John Ferrell: Well, I must tell you that I found Strategic Coach to be very liberating in a lot of ways. It really is an ecosystem for self-improvement. I had these secret thoughts for a long time, but it was not until I got into this ecosystem that I was able to express some of the things I was thinking in private.

Dan Sullivan: *You also saw a lot of examples of how people package things.*
John Ferrell: Absolutely. That's one of the reasons I've enjoyed Strategic Coach so much—it gives you the opportunity to be around really successful people who also think outside the box.

Dan Sullivan: *What a totally different model for the legal profession you have created.*
John Ferrell: Thanks, Dan. You know, I turn fifty this year, and so many of my colleagues who have reached that age are really burned out by law. They have spent their careers in courthouses, yelling and screaming. They've got high stress and high blood pressure. I love what I'm doing and I cannot wait to get into the office every morning. I mean that sincerely —this is a wonderful way to spend my career.

For contact details on the Strategic IP Process, please see page 214.

Value Creation

Ingredient 4
Value Creation

The idea of "value creation" is a hot topic in organizational and management circles today. Virtually all industries are caught in a "commoditization trap" where survival and success increasingly depend upon selling products and services at lower prices. The more that price cutting is on consumers' minds, the more necessary it is to offer them something extra to differentiate yourself from all the other price cutters. Everywhere, in every marketplace, there is a greater need to create and provide greater value around every kind of commodity sale.

All Unique Process entrepreneurs operate in commoditized industries, but they never have to resort to price cutting. Their so-called competitors do, but they never do. Tony and Mary Miller charge higher than the going rate on all of their janitorial contracts. How are they able to achieve this?

The answer is that they and our other entrepreneurs operating in Unique Processes provide much higher levels of value in all of their relationships. They are masters of value creation. David Allen's detailing service for private jets is so good at providing an entirely different kind of marketplace experience that their clients seldom make price a deciding factor. Their clients and customers think about them in a completely different way.

Philip Tirone gets full commissions in a mortgage industry where competing brokers are slashing their rates. John

Ferrell achieves higher fees and profit margins than the vast majority of intellectual property lawyers. In the clientele's mind, these entrepreneurs are in a class by themselves. As a result, other companies seldom get the opportunity to compete for the business.

Clients so satisfied they become unpaid salespeople.
Here's a personal experience that spotlights the unique value creation advantage that Unique Process entrepreneurs have over any competition. My company, Strategic Coach, uses John Ferrell's services. We are taking advantage of his Unique Process, and it has been of great value to us. It will be even more valuable in the future. John's legal concepts and strategies have revolutionized our thinking about how we package, position, and protect ourselves in the marketplace. We are also using John's firm to file our patent applications that emerge from the strategic thinking we are doing inside of his process.

When I tell entrepreneurs who are in our Program about John's approach, they always ask how much it costs. When I tell them, and even though it is more than what other intellectual property lawyers charge for their conventional services, the response is always the same: *"Oh, that's nothing." "That's cheap." "Do you think he'll work with me?"*

Not only do the clients of all these Unique Process entrepreneurs pay premium prices for these services, they are deeply appreciative of the quality experience and comprehensive solutions they receive for their money. As our own experience with John indicates, there is a great desire on the part of clients and customers to become enthusiastic, unpaid marketers and salespeople for these unique value creators.

Where does the value creation come from? How do the Unique Process entrepreneurs continually develop and

provide uniquely valuable solutions to their clients that put them in a class of their own?

There are two answers. First, all of these entrepreneurs already had powerful value creation attitudes and abilities before they joined Strategic Coach and developed their Unique Processes. They had already achieved considerable success because they instinctively knew how to differentiate themselves from price-cutting competition. What the structure of the Unique Process provides is a way of creating value as the central, most lucrative activity of their business. It takes their natural instinct toward value creation and makes it standard operating procedure. While other companies that are entirely commodity-based can create new value only rarely and with great difficulty, the Unique Process enables these entrepreneurs to do it every day as an ordinary, enjoyable activity.

Providing valuable direction, confidence, and capability.

The second answer to the questions above is that all of these entrepreneurs have internalized a value creation formula in Strategic Coach that goes by the acronym "LRC," which stands for leadership, relationship, and creativity. This formula was derived from years of observing how successful entrepreneurs differentiated themselves in the marketplace. In every instance, the differentiation occurred as a result of LRC. There are three things that consumers value in today's world more than anything else. They value someone giving them a clear sense of direction in a world of confusing choices. This is leadership. They value someone providing them with the personal confidence they need to make important decisions and take effective actions, sometimes under difficult, isolating conditions. This is relationship. And they value gaining new capabilities where old approaches and methods no longer work as well, or at all. This is creativity.

Value that can't be obtained anywhere else, at any price.

As entrepreneurs develop their Unique Processes, their ability to provide leadership, relationship, and creativity continually increases. This occurs in response to their clients' most pressing problems, best opportunities, and greatest ambitions. As we have already seen in the interviews with Richard Rossi, Tony and Mary Miller, and John Ferrell, their Unique Processes enable them to provide their clients and customers with a powerful sense of new direction, confidence, and capability that is impossible to obtain anywhere else, at any price.

Our next interview is with Joe Polish, who has not only created an "easy, lucrative, and fun" business for himself, he has innovated practically an entirely new industry where none existed before. The amount of value creation that he provides to his customers and clients is extraordinary. Anyone who meets Joe is immediately impressed by his high energy, insatiable curiosity, creative mind, impish humor, and generous spirit. After you read the interview, you'll agree that he is a true value creator.

Joe Polish
Piranha Marketing™

Joe Polish used the lessons he learned turning his struggling carpet-cleaning business into a hugely successful venture, to transform the entire carpet-cleaning industry — and to create Piranha Marketing™, one of the world's most successful and effective marketing programs for small business owners in any industry.

Dan Sullivan: *It's a pleasure to be talking with Joe Polish. Joe is an extraordinary entrepreneur who began his career as a carpet cleaner and has now transformed into a global marketing guru. I want to begin, Joe, by asking how you first got started in the carpet-cleaning business, because I know that carpet cleaning isn't exactly the most glamorous business out there.*

Joe Polish: (Laughing) You're certainly right about that, Dan. Nobody grows up saying, "I want to be a carpet cleaner." I got my start, though, in an even less glamorous business: newspaper delivery. By the age of thirteen, I was going door to door delivering newspapers and selling newspaper subscriptions. I recognized that the way you make something happen in the world is by selling things. Lo and behold, I sold more newspaper subscriptions to *The Arizona Republic* than any other seller, and I was rewarded with a trip to Disneyland. So I like to think of that experience as my first introduction to the "results economy."

Dan Sullivan: *In what part of Arizona were you living?*

Joe Polish: We moved around a lot, primarily in the Phoenix metro area. I also lived in parts of Texas and New Mexico. My mother died when I was four years old, and my father was really tormented. He could never settle down. Anyway, I went to community college for a few years but never got a degree. So I wasn't very "employable" in the conventional sense, and I guess that's what drove me to carpet cleaning.

■ *Dan, you like to say that the two things any aspiring entrepreneur needs are ignorance and courage, and I was fortunate to have large quantities of both.* ■

Dan Sullivan: *How old were you at the time?*

Joe Polish: About twenty-two years old. I had started a business selling advertising space on the outside of phone-book covers. When that business failed, I didn't know where to turn, and a friend of mine told me about a carpet-cleaning company that was doing $600,000 in business each year. With only $1,500 left in my pocket, I put everything into a portable steam-cleaning machine and some cleaning chemicals, while printing business cards that said "professional carpet cleaner." This is a business that doesn't have a lot of regulations or barriers to entry. So almost overnight I became a professional carpet cleaner.

Dan Sullivan: *You were a business owner.*

Joe Polish: I was. I mean it certainly wasn't anything to write home about, but at least I had a sense of ownership. Dan, you like to say that the two things any aspiring entrepreneur needs are ignorance and courage, and I was fortunate to have large quantities of both.

Dan Sullivan: *Was it rough sailing in those first few months?*

Joe Polish: You bet. I was bumbling around, going door-to-door, handing out business cards and trying to make sales. Nothing was automated. My gross per month was about $2,000, which wasn't enough to cover overhead, so I was in the negative. I was basically paying to work. And this went on for an entire year. Without credit cards, I wouldn't have been able to sustain the business.

Dan Sullivan: *But you were using this time to learn the tricks of the trade.*

Joe Polish: I went out and got certified and acquired more training. I thought the solution to my problems was to become a better cleaner and learn more about the technical aspects of cleaning. But then came a defining moment. I was fortunate enough to go jet skiing with an old friend from high school. One of the people on the trip was a multimillionaire real estate investor. So I had the opportunity to sit down and talk business with this guy on the tailgate of a pickup truck. I asked him for some recommendations on the kinds of businesses I could go into to make a lot of money, because I certainly wasn't making any money in carpet cleaning. He responded, "Are there other people in the carpet-cleaning industry who make a lot of money?" I told him that a few companies out there are making over a million dollars. So he turned to me and said, "Well, it appears that there's nothing wrong with the business you're in, so there must be something wrong with you." And he warned that if I tried to go into another business, I'd waste between six months and two years getting the training and technical skills, while repeating the same bad business habits that had made me a failure in carpet cleaning. His point was that learning the technical side of an industry isn't enough. You have to learn how to run a successful business.

Dan Sullivan: *This experience must have been a real wakeup call.*

Joe Polish: I'll never forget the conversation. You know, at this point I had been in the business almost two and a half years. I came in to the meeting with somewhat of a victim mentality, an entitlement attitude. And I left with a healthy dose of humility. I figured I'd make it work. Here I was, a young guy in the greatest country in the world, with full use of my limbs and my brain, and my whole future in front of me. So I stopped feeling sorry for myself and went to work.

Dan Sullivan: *You started focusing on the marketing dimension.*
Joe Polish: Exactly. I realized that my problems were marketing problems, so my solutions needed to be marketing solutions. A business friend introduced me to a newsletter published by a wild and crazy guy named Gary Halbert, who also was brilliant at writing sales and advertising copy. The newsletter wasn't very long at all, but it was very valuable. And I started to realize that smart people would rather pay a thousand dollars for ten pages of useful information, than ten dollars for three hundred pages of junk. That's because ultimately the most expensive information in the world is always bad information.

Dan Sullivan: *So you subscribed to the newsletter.*
Joe Polish: I subscribed, and from that point forward, I was exposed to this whole world called direct response marketing. People usually think that marketing is about getting their name out and establishing a brand identity through advertising. In contrast, direct response marketing is focused on developing

I realized that if I marketed correctly, everybody I talked to would already be pre-interested, pre-motivated, pre-qualified, and pre-disposed to do business with me.

marketplace messages that have a response mechanism. In other words, you're always asking people to do something and respond in some way. As I learned more, I started to grasp the crucial distinction between "sales" and "marketing." Up until that time, the only thing I was doing in my carpet-cleaning business was sales. I was literally going door to door trying to get sales. In reality, I was basically begging people to give me business. Marketing, in contrast, is all about positioning. I realized that if I marketed correctly, everybody I talked to would already be pre-interested, pre-motivated, pre-qualified, and pre-disposed to do business with me.

Dan Sullivan: *That's when you started marketing through free recorded messages.*
Joe Polish: Yes. I created a kind of consumer awareness guide in print instead of a brochure, and I used an education-based marketing system for carpet cleaning: things like the "eight mistakes to avoid when choosing a carpet cleaner." I put all of this information into a ten-minute recording on how to choose a carpet cleaner. Then I put a message on the back of my business card that said "Warning: Don't call any carpet cleaner until you listen to this 24-hour free recorded message." Whenever I met new people or gave them a business card, I'd remind them to call this free recorded message. Of course, at the end of the message, I gave my listeners contact information, so it did have a more traditional marketing component. But in no sense was I pressuring people to do business with me. I was basically giving them free access to information on how to choose the right company so people could feel confident they were making an informed and intelligent decision.

Dan Sullivan: *And you were developing relationships and gaining visibility in the process.*
Joe Polish: Exactly. Whenever I met somebody, I left them

with a ten-minute, perfectly articulate salesperson that they could call and listen to 24 hours a day, seven days a week. It cost me 20 bucks a month and did a much better job promoting my service than if I were to physically conduct ten-minute, face-to-face meetings with all of these people. What I realized is that through these kinds of direct response marketing techniques, you can reach thousands, even millions, of people with minimal effort. In a six-month period, I took a carpet-cleaning company that was only grossing $2,000 a month to grossing over $12,000 per month.

Dan Sullivan: *You developed a system for making your business exponentially more efficient.*
Joe Polish: That's the way I looked at it. From this point forward, every time I was exposed to something new, I thought about what kind of process or system I could develop to make it more effective. So, for example, I developed something called The Carpet Audit™ that was used during home visits. Whenever I visited a home, I'd evaluate the condition of the carpet. How many people are living in the home? How many pets do they have? Does anybody smoke? In other words, what factors are impacting the current condition of the carpet? I acquired this information through a four-page questionnaire. So I was able to give people a personalized Carpet Audit that diagnosed the particular steps involved with cleaning their carpet. It was a huge differentiator.

Dan Sullivan: *Joe, at this point you're becoming more successful as a carpet cleaner. Let's move on to the next growth stage. When did you start realizing that you could be extraordinarily valuable to other cleaners?*
Joe Polish: Well, it sort of started as an accident. I was at a carpet-cleaning conference, and there were some industry bigwigs peddling advice. Most of the advice wasn't very good.

One speaker was advocating 40 percent discounts and actually calling this the most effective marketing strategy. I got around to telling people about my success with free recorded messages, and some carpet cleaners became interested. I told them, "I'll sell you the script of the free recorded message and the template for a Yellow Pages ad for $250." Two cleaners took me up on the offer, and one guy turned this $250 investment into more than $62,000 in new revenue in one year. I started to think, "Hey, maybe I'm onto something. How do I sell this to other carpet cleaners?"

Dan Sullivan: This was basically a marketing challenge.
Joe Polish: Exactly. You know, for a while, my goal was simply to build the largest carpet-cleaning company in Phoenix. Then I realized that my Unique Ability, what I really love, is marketing. I love the fact that you can dramatically increase customer response just by changing the words on a business card or in an advertisement. So I ran an ad in the regional section of a trade magazine. This was sort of a dry run, and I got a huge response. Then I went about creating a manual called *105 Money Making Marketing Strategies*™ for carpet cleaners. I recorded some audio, wrote some booklets, and started selling courses to carpet cleaners. The first year, in 1994, I sold $250,000 worth of knowledge products to carpet cleaners. By the third year I had sold over a million dollars worth of these things. Eventually, as the years went by, I would end up selling over $12 million in knowledge products to carpet cleaners.

Dan Sullivan: You became a major player in the industry.
Joe Polish: I gained over 5,000 companies who loved my stuff and were transforming their businesses, along with some enemies who found me disruptive because they were married to stupid, archaic ways of doing things. But I kept going. I packaged more strategies and DVDs. I created more training programs. And

I joined Strategic Coach, which was, of course, incredibly valuable in terms of keeping me focused on innovation.

Dan Sullivan: *Why don't we talk a little more about the marketing strategies that you're teaching, because I know that over the years, you've developed a really effective set of strategies.*
Joe Polish: Sure. As you know, my company is called Piranha Marketing, and all of our intellectual capital is focused around what we call ELF Marketing™. The goal is to help clients create a business that's Easy, Lucrative, and Fun (ELF). So there are seven key strategies. Obviously, the first is the use of free recorded messages. Second, business owners need to have a powerful sales letter that clones their most effective sales presentation in a reproducible form. Third, they should create a monthly newsletter for clients. I'm a big believer in contacting your clients monthly. Fourth, they need to have a system for utilizing referrals in a strategic way. Fifth, they need to be adept at using testimonials as marketing material. Sixth, they need to offer a powerful, 100% money-back guarantee on everything they sell. Finally, they should never run an ad a second time if it doesn't work the first time.

Dan Sullivan: *That's great, Joe. What strikes me is that ELF Marketing and the strategies you've laid out clearly hold relevance for all kinds of industries beyond carpet cleaning.*
Joe Polish: Absolutely. You know, nobody looks forward to getting their carpet cleaned. It's one of those necessary evils that comes with owning the stuff. So I have to teach people how to effectively sell—in an easy, lucrative, and fun way—a service that is actually highly unpleasant for consumers. Think about it. Carpet cleaning is messy, it's disruptive, it forces people to leave their home for a few hours. So I like to think that if my strategies work in this business, then they're bound to work in any business that's even a little bit more sexy and exciting than carpet cleaning.

Dan Sullivan: Where did you branch off?

Joe Polish: I started licensing my marketing programs to industries like home remodeling, pest control, auto sales, HVAC, printing, jewelry, and painting, to name just a few. I had people pay me $35,000 upfront with ongoing royalties just to license my "105 Strategies" manual.

Dan Sullivan: You also started coaching, right?

Joe Polish: That's right. In 1997, I started doing teleseminar coaching, and I ended up doing $250,000 of sales on a 75-minute phone call that was properly positioned. That led to the development of our Platinum Plus Program, which includes a variety of membership services. Members get access to all Piranha marketing strategies and the ability to utilize those strategies in their own business. They get access to a client newsletter sent every month. They get access to a variety of recorded audio interviews, such as our Genius Network Interview Series, which I'll talk about in a moment. They get monthly coaching calls, where they can network with other members. And a lot of other services are included. Platinum Plus membership currently starts at $17,000 per year, and we also offer Gold and Silver packages. Right now we have over 4,100 carpet cleaners that are active Piranha members, and, of course, we continue to work with people in other industries.

Dan Sullivan: Could you talk about some success stories, because I'm sure you have a lot of clients who've experienced phenomenal growth after applying your strategies?

Joe Polish: Sure. First of all, one of the things I decided to do when Platinum Plus was starting was to run a contest. I had a Jaguar convertible that was given to me by my client Bill Phillips, the author of *Body for Life*. In 2001, I decided to give it away in a spokesperson contest to the top performer in my Platinum Plus group. The result was a real competition among

> *I had one guy from a small town in Nebraska who was actually losing money in the business and thinking about quitting. Within one year of joining my Platinum Plus Program, he did over $1.3 million in revenue.*

members to see who could experience the best results over a three-month period of time. I had one guy from a small town in Nebraska who was actually losing money in the business and thinking about quitting. Within one year of joining my Platinum Plus Program, he did over $1.3 million in revenue. Guess what? He won the contest. I have another client named Steve Cameron, who was stuck with the same revenue for 22 years in the business. After four years in my program he quadrupled his revenue. So we continue to use the contest model, and it's been very successful as a motivator. But, of course, it all comes down to using those marketing strategies effectively.

Dan Sullivan: *At what point did you start running Super Conferences for thousands of industry professionals?*
Joe Polish: Twelve years ago, we started doing these conferences for carpet cleaners, and we called them Boot Camps. In 2007, it became a Super Conference open to all entrepreneurs, and we had over 700 people attend. These three-day events allow participants to network and also learn more about our marketing strategies. At the 2007 event alone, we generated over $2 million in revenue. This first Super Conference featured some amazing speakers, like Sir Richard Branson, Bill Phillips, Tim Ferriss, Cameron Johnson, Dr. Edward Hallowell, and more. The whole objective of the Super Conference is to help our participants develop what we call an ELF Life.

Dan Sullivan: *Joe, it's so exciting to hear about your progress, and it gets greater every year. Let's talk a bit about The Genius Network, because I know that this is a very important program for you.*

Joe Polish: (Laughing) It all started when I was past deadline to write and mail my monthly Piranha Marketing newsletter to clients. Instead I interviewed a sales expert and sent the audio out to my clients. They loved it, and we started recording these interviews on a regular basis. Eventually, we formed The Genius Network™. I started seeking out people, from any background, who were interesting or had some wisdom that they could impart. I've since done over 150 interviews with some of the most amazing people on the planet. Our clients can subscribe to the interviews, and they're included as part of some of our membership programs. So it has really become a goldmine of wisdom that our clients can tap into.

Dan Sullivan: *I know you also have a strong presence on Nightingale-Conant.*

Joe Polish: I was talking with Vic Conant, and I told him I could dramatically reduce the refunds at Nightingale by using a "stick strategy" follow-up system. I would charge him a fee for creating that system. Or, they could do a marketing program with me, and I would be protected in terms of royalties. Long story short, they picked me up, and I've now got the number-one-selling marketing program at Nightingale-Conant.

Dan Sullivan: *Joe, as we talk here in 2008, it's just amazing how far you've come.*

Joe Polish: Thanks, Dan. You know, back in 1994, I was selling consumer awareness guides for $250. Now, I charge people $20,000 per day for personal consulting, and I'm working with some huge companies like Wells Fargo and Esselte, which owns Pendaflex. Over the next year, I'll be putting my first mass-market book out. I've started a $25,000-per-person membership group for information marketers, and I'm starting a group next year at $100,000 per person.

Dan Sullivan: *And you've done it all with relatively low overhead.*

Joe Polish: That's right. Here at Piranha Marketing, we only employ about eight people at our headquarters in Tempe, . Arizona. My marketing systems don't require a large sales force. We rely on a lot of referrals, automated systems, and, of course, our web presence at *www.joepolish.com.* We've set it up in such a way that the expenses are minimal and the profit margins are very healthy.

Dan Sullivan: *Joe, you started out with a carpet-cleaning company. Now, carpet cleaning is only one of your distribution channels. What aspirations do you have, because you've got what appears to be an incredible future sketched out?*

Joe Polish: First of all, I need to continue building on my strength, which is the ELF Marketing system. When it comes to carpet cleaning, there's not a major franchise in the industry that hasn't invested in my stuff and become a Piranha member. The best information in the world for marketing and promoting in the cleaning industry is sitting in my office. There isn't a major phone book in any city in the United States that doesn't have some derivative of my advertising techniques, from multiple different industries, with free recorded messages running. But I'm also looking forward to new opportunities, such as expanding The Genius Network, because I just love doing it. Even if I didn't get paid, it'd be worthwhile, because there's nothing more useful than sitting down and having discussions with bright people. It's really taught me the power of asking questions.

Another real passion of mine is in the area of consumer advocacy. The carpet-cleaning industry is notorious for having a lot of scam artists. I was actually one of the first people to start exposing some of their bait-and-switch techniques on a national level. I've been interviewed on 20/20 with Barbara Walters, and I've been on local television four different times teaching consumers how to avoid getting ripped off by unethical companies. Moving forward, my goal is to transform the way consumers find businesses. On my website, I've created a section called "Joe Polish Recommends." This is a million-dollar Rolodex that features hundreds of professionals from a variety of industries. Only professionals that I have personally done business with, or that were recommended to me with the highest regard, are featured.

Dan Sullivan: What about Ethical Services?
Joe Polish: Ethical Services is an extremely exciting consumer educational and awareness network that I'm developing. By going to the website at EthicalServices.com, consumers can gain access to a network of 30,000 professional carpet cleaners. People can search by zip code and see a listing of carpet cleaners in their area, along with the ratings that previous customers have given them. Every cleaning company that joins the Ethical Services network has to agree to a member code of ethics characterized by only the highest standards of professional conduct. And this site will be expanded to numerous service industries beyond cleaning.

Dan Sullivan: Is there a business model attached to Ethical Services?
Joe Polish: Well, of course it's valuable as a networking and marketing tool. It gets my name out there with small business owners who want to join the network. One of the perks I'm able to offer my Platinum Plus and Gold members is a premium listing

> *Best of all, it feels like I'm just getting started.*
> *I've yet to make even a fraction of the contribu-*
> *tion I'm capable of making in the world.*

on Ethical Services, assuming, of course, that they agree to the member code of conduct. But I really don't want Ethical Services to become part of Joe Polish Associates. I want to maintain its independence as just an extraordinarily valuable consumer educational resource. Of course, there might be some additional opportunities down the line that we can leverage, but at the moment we're donating most of the revenue to charity.

My other big initiative is to apply some of my marketing skills and networking skills to create a social network for people suffering from attention deficit disorder and alcohol, drug, or behavioral addictions. I've dealt with some of these issues throughout my life, not to mention being a true workaholic, which is one of the worst kinds of addiction. A philosopher once said that the last thing human beings ever give up is their suffering. And I'm just convinced that twelve-step programs and other social support networks are the best systems out there for relieving human suffering among addicts.

Dan Sullivan: *I can see the passion coming through in every-thing you're talking about.*
Joe Polish: I've been fortunate enough to acquire some financial freedom, and now I'm in a position to really have a positive impact on other people. Being a marketer isn't just about selling products. I've got these God-given talents in the area of marketing, and I want to use them to promote causes that can help others. When I go to the grave, I don't want people to say, "That guy taught more cleaners to suck dirt out of carpet."

Sure, that's one thing I do, but it doesn't capture the whole person.

Dan Sullivan: *I get a sense, Joe, that if you didn't focus on those big goals, if you didn't carry the attitude that "I'm going to contribute to the world," then you wouldn't be having the impact on the marketplace that you're having. It's fueling your fire.*
Joe Polish: Absolutely.

Dan Sullivan: *Joe, it's just remarkable how much you've accomplished. How old are you?*
Joe Polish: Thirty-nine.

Dan Sullivan: *Thirty-nine years old. Wow! How does it feel to have achieved so much at such a young age?*
Joe Polish: Dan, I can't even describe it. Sixteen years ago I was a broke carpet cleaner surviving on credit cards, and next thing you know I'm flying around on private jets, attending the Oscars, charging $20,000 for a day of consulting. I go out to dinner with people like Richard Branson and interview amazing people on a regular basis. I've helped thousands of carpet cleaners transform their future, and I'm in a position to help millions of consumers get ethical treatment in the marketplace. Best of all, it feels like I'm just getting started. I've yet to make even a fraction of the contribution I'm capable of making in the world.

For contact details on Piranha Marketing, please see page 215.

INGREDIENT 5

Transformation

Transformation

In today's marketplace, many consumers are looking to *transform* their situations. In other words, they aren't satisfied with incremental improvements; they want dramatic changes for the better. They want breakthroughs and quantum leaps.

When Joe Polish works with the carpet cleaners who join his program, the first objective is to increase their revenues and profits by three times or more in a matter of a year. But it's more than that. As they go through Joe's Unique Process, these individuals take a jump in terms of being strategic, ethical, professional business people. They are transformed, and this differentiates them from those carpet cleaners who give the industry a bad reputation for dishonest marketing practices and low-quality work.

Clients want to become new, better, and different people. When John Ferrell takes on an entrepreneurial startup as a client, the purpose of their working partnership is to create a "marketplace monopoly" within three years. But while this is occurring, these entrepreneurs and their companies are transformed in their thinking about innovation, packaging, and marketing. They become completely different, and much more strategic, enterprises.

Both of these examples are in alignment with an emerging trend: the growth of the transformational economy. When consumers engage with companies in the marketplace, they obviously want much bigger and better practical results—but they also want a greater sense of direction, confidence, and capability. They want highly enjoyable transformative experiences in which they as individuals, and as organizations, are transformed.

Richard Rossi reports that thousands of parents and teachers thank him for the "transformations" they see in the top students who come back from the programs that his company designs and provides. But it is not just the students who are transformed. The larger transformational experience has enormous impact on Richard's organization, participating specialists, guest speakers, and the parents and teachers who make it possible for the students to attend. Everyone comes away from an Envision EMI program with a heightened sense of their own aspirations and capabilities.

A powerful transformational economy is emerging.
I believe that this yearning for personal and organizational transformation constitutes an entirely new sector of the global economy that is only now being recognized. And this emerging reality of the "transformational sector" requires an entirely new kind of business structure to serve it.

That structure is the Unique Process. The very essence of the Unique Process is transformational. It enables there to be a continual transformation of clients' most pressing issues: the things that most worry them, the things that most excite them, and the things they feel most confident about. All of these are related to their most ambitious desires for the future. This is one part of the transformation that takes place inside of the Unique Process. The other part is provided by the entrepreneurs and their teams. Their wisdom, knowledge, capabilities, and methods are transformed as they create new solutions for the specific problems and requirements of their clientele. This kind of transformative process is directly opposite to the experience of being offered only commoditized products and services. More consumers in more industries are increasingly tired and frustrated by being treated in a commoditized fashion. They want their marketplace experiences, in all aspects of their lives, to be transformational.

Knowing what to do, and being the only one who can.
Each of the entrepreneurs we feature in this book promises transformative experiences and results from his or her Unique Process. There are two reasons for this. One, they know that they can fulfill the promise, and, two, they know that no one else in their industry can match what they do.

Gary Boomer puts it this way: *"There are a lot of technology consultants in the accounting industry, but none of them can provide anything close to what happens in our Technology Circles. When our clients experience our Unique Process, they not only become smarter professionals, they become better leaders and more cooperative human beings. In the end, their increased expertise with technology, while significant, is a small part of the transformation they go through, both as individuals and organizations."*

Tony and Mary Miller talk about the profound changes that their employees from Latin America, Africa, and Eastern Europe undergo simply by working at Jancoa: *"These people come to the U.S. just hoping for the possibility of a better life for their children. What they get from working with us is a whole new life for themselves. They transform in positive ways that would have been inconceivable in their home countries. What happens to them is beyond their greatest hopes."*

But the transformation doesn't stop there. The large companies that use Jancoa's services discover that this janitorial company has better trained, more motivated, and more productive workers than they have. They want to know the secret, and Tony and Mary are happy to share it with them. Many of these firms have adapted The Dream Manager program to bring about similar transformations in their workforces.

As Tony and Mary mention in their interview, one of the largest cleaning companies in America has licensed one of their Unique Processes in order to improve the quality of their services and their customer retention. When this licensing program is fully implemented over the next several years, it will bring about a profound transformation in the way this company does business in the marketplace.

Our next Unique Process entrepreneur is Philip Tirone, who is not only transforming his clients and the other mortgage brokers in his industry, he has plans to transform the entire U.S. economy based on millions of Americans achieving credit score literacy. Knowing Philip and his track record, I feel certain he is going to have a huge national impact.

Philip Tirone

7 Steps to a 720® Credit Score

In his early days as a Santa Monica mortgage broker, Philip Tirone was working two headsets to make 45,000 cold calls a year. It didn't take him long to figure out that this might produce great results, but it didn't lend itself to longevity. And when an embarrassing denial at his bank as a result of his credit score produced an "ah-ha" moment, Philip created 7 Steps to a 720® Credit Score, a Unique Process that totally transformed how he provides value for his clients. It is now transforming his industry, and Philip sees its potential to impact the U.S. economy in a positive and powerful

Dan Sullivan: Philip, the way this works for us and for the readers is to begin with a little history. How did you get started in the mortgage industry?
Philip Tirone: I went to college at Arizona State University. And during college, I got my real estate license and started working for a developer. After graduation, they moved me up to Prescott, Arizona, where I started selling modular homes to senior citizens.

Dan Sullivan: Sophisticated trailers.
Philip Tirone: Exactly. I joined the Rotary Club, and they chose me for a two-month trip to India. When I came back from India, I realized how much more there was to life than selling modular homes in Prescott.

Dan Sullivan: Not very exciting for a recent college graduate.
Philip Tirone: You hit the nail on the head. I promised a Rotary friend that I would be gone in six months, even though I had no idea where I was going. He introduced me to some of his friends in Santa Monica. I started meeting people and was in awe of the big city.

Dan Sullivan: *How did you get your first mortgage job?*
Philip Tirone: I came out to California with $25,000 in the bank and no idea where I was going to get work. Finally, I found a mortgage company, but they wouldn't return my calls. I ended up faxing them a letter saying, "Hey, I'm going to be out in Los Angeles on Thursday. I'll meet you at either 3:00 or 4:00 in the afternoon. I'll call your assistant tomorrow at 11:00 to find out which time you want. By the way, enjoy the fruit." I had these pears flown in from Oregon.

Dan Sullivan: *So you finally persuaded a company representative to meet with you.*
Philip Tirone: The hiring manager said he was glad to meet me, but told me all the real estate offices were closed to new mortgage brokers. "How in the world are you going to get in front of people?" he asked. I said, very calmly, "The same way I got in front of you." I was hired on the spot.

Dan Sullivan: *Not too bad for a day's work.*
Philip Tirone: I was certainly excited, but I really knew nothing about what I was doing. I went through $25,000 in three months. I remember being in my rent-controlled apartment calling my dad and saying, "Dad, I'm out of money. I don't know what to do. Have I failed?" And he said, "Phil, you will have failed when you stop swinging at the ball. Just keep swinging."

Dan Sullivan: *And then you got a hit.*
Philip Tirone: Sure enough, when times are lowest, opportunity comes. I met a guy who was a personal coach. He said, "I'll teach you how to make money, piece of cake." Basically, he taught me how to cold call. I started cold calling with double headsets. In 1998, I dialed 45,000 times, contacted 15,000 people, and became number one in the company. Obviously, when you've dialed that many times, you get some business.

Dan Sullivan: *What kind of production are we talking about?*
Philip Tirone: In terms of personal income I was making about $150,000 to $175,000, which was four times what I was making in Prescott. But industry-wide, it was nothing. I just happened to be in a small shop. Then I discovered a ranking of the top 15 mortgage brokers in the country. Five of them happened to be in Los Angeles, and their volume was just huge. These people were doing 20 times what I was doing.

Dan Sullivan: *So you realized there's a whole different world out there in the mortgage industry.*
Philip Tirone: Right. And I wanted to join that world. I called up some of these companies and asked if I could pick their brain for $500 an hour. When we sat down, they turned off the recorder, pushed the money aside, and said, "Look, we're not doing an interview. We want you to work for us." So I jumped at the opportunity to be with a bigger company with better resources.

Dan Sullivan: *What year was this?*
Philip Tirone: This was 1998. From 1998 to 2001, I kept working my way up. But my strategy was still based on making more calls than the other guy. People asked, "How are you going to increase your production here?" And my answer was simple: "I'm going to be on the phone an extra hour a day."

Dan Sullivan: *You were basically a 24/7 guy.*
Philip Tirone: Oh, yeah. Back then, I never took vacation. All I did was work. But that was my badge of honor. That was how I identified myself—as someone who would out-work anybody. You know, there were times when I'd be driving to the office at four in the morning. I'd stop at a red light, barely awake, and there were some young guys in another car just finishing up their night of partying. And I thought to myself, "Look at this. What a competitive advantage I have. I'm

starting my day. These guys are just ending their night drunk."

Dan Sullivan: *Of course that kind of lifestyle doesn't lend itself to a lot of longevity.*
Philip Tirone: Absolutely not. So it was a really important wake-up call when I joined Strategic Coach in 2001 and started learning the importance of free time. The truth of the matter is that it wasn't easy for me to change. Working hard has always been a part of my identity, and it still is. I continue to work a solid 12-hour day, but now I do it five days a week as opposed to seven.

Dan Sullivan: *Philip, you've got a great wife, you've got a child, and you wouldn't have even been in a position to meet someone when you started the Coach program—unless you met her at three or four in the morning when you were driving to work.*
Philip Tirone: You're right. I was expecting to meet my future wife at daily Mass, because that was the only time I ever took off from work.

Dan Sullivan: *Another thing that you were struggling with in the workshops was whether to continue in the mortgage industry.*
Philip Tirone: Dan, I remember coming up to you and saying, "I'm not excited about the mortgage business. I want to do something else." At which point, you gave me some of the best advice ever. You said, "Phil, your position in the loan business will evolve. Let it evolve. Don't take all this experience, all this knowledge, and throw it all away." And those were prophetic words, because I can't imagine myself in a more exciting place than I am in right now.

Dan Sullivan: *That's great, Philip. Why don't we talk about what you've created, your Unique Process—7 Steps to a 720 Credit Score. What I've found, Philip, is that most people are just clueless about the whole credit-scoring process and the* *role of credit in their lives. So why don't you talk about some of the common misperceptions people have?*

Philip Tirone: Sure, I'd love to. First of all, I can't tell you how many times people have come up to me and said, "Oh, I've got to have a perfect credit score. I've been paying my bills on time each month. As a matter of fact, I pay them in full each month. I don't even carry a balance." Unfortunately, the credit-scoring process doesn't work that way. Only 35 percent of your credit score is based on whether you pay the bills on time.

Dan Sullivan: You've had a personal encounter with this system, haven't you?

Philip Tirone: One day, I walked into the bank to deposit a check. I was overdrawn on my checking account, so the teller offered me overdraft protection, but had to run my credit report. I thought to myself, "Well, I pay my bills on time. It must be perfect." To my great surprise, she said I'd been denied. It was really an embarrassing moment, and I actually looked around to make sure nobody had overheard. Nine months later, I bought a home. Because I had a credit score in the low 600s, I was overpaying each month by $600 on the mortgage. It just hit me like a ton of bricks.

Dan Sullivan: And that's coming from a mortgage broker.

Philip Tirone: Exactly. I mean, here I was, a mortgage broker, and I didn't even understand the credit system. That's when I decided to learn everything there is to know about this issue.

Dan Sullivan: And you started developing the 7 Steps to a 720 Credit Score brand.

Philip Tirone: That's right. As I became more and more knowledgeable, the question was how to package my wisdom in the form of intellectual capital. So I decided to put my ideas in book form. I hired a ghostwriter, and we wrote *7 Steps to a 720 Credit Score.*

Statistically speaking, 50 percent of Americans have a credit score below 720. So we're talking about over 100 million Americans who have a bad credit score, which could be impacting their lifestyle.

Dan Sullivan: *Now at this time you were still in the transaction business. But you had a tool that no other mortgage broker had. What kind of impact did the book have on your relationships with clients?*

Philip Tirone: What I noticed, Dan, is that anyone who came to me with a credit score below 720 related to me in a completely different way. Having my book in hand immediately distinguished me, and my commissions on those transactions went way up. Meanwhile, real estate agents throughout the city started referring people over to me.

Dan Sullivan: *How frequent is it for people to have a credit score below 720?*

Philip Tirone: Statistically speaking, 50 percent of Americans have a credit score below 720. So we're talking about over 100 million Americans who have a credit score that could be impacting their lifestyle. Not to mention the fact that 80 percent of people, even those with a credit score above 720, have an error on their credit report. If this error isn't caught, it can send a score to below 720 before you know it.

Dan Sullivan: *This isn't a rich/poor thing, is it?*

Philip Tirone: Absolutely not. It transcends income, race, whatever. I've seen people with millions of dollars in the bank and credit scores below 720.

Dan Sullivan: *Why are so many otherwise savvy people in the dark about the credit score process?*

Philip Tirone: You know, Dan, Doug Andrew wrote a foreword for my book. And he puts it this way: Imagine needing to take a test. The test determines how much you're going to pay on your next home purchase. You want to do well on the test. But you can't study for the test because the credit bureaus don't release the scoring techniques. The only part they release is 22 vague categories that are said to impact your credit score. Now, suppose you get a mediocre score on the test and are paying an extra $300 per month. You want to improve your results, but nobody's there to tell you why you did poorly in the first place. It's just unfair in so many ways.

Dan Sullivan: *But, of course, you've developed a strategy to help people improve.*

Philip Tirone: You know, there are a lot of books on credit. They'll teach you to do things that have no real impact on your credit score. You might spend ten hours working and only improve your credit score by one point. 7 Steps to 720® only focuses on the seven most important items. The strategy is presented in a way that's clear and doesn't seem overwhelming.

Dan Sullivan: *Why is 720 such an important number?*

Philip Tirone: For whatever reason, the mortgage world has made 720 the magic number. When you have a 720 credit score, many banks don't even need to see large portions of your application. You'll definitely get the best rate.

Dan Sullivan: *Now at this point,* 7 Steps to 720 *had become a huge asset to your commodity business. When did you begin to see another possibility for making a complete living within the realm of intellectual capital?*

Philip Tirone: It got to the point where other mortgage companies wanted to give my book out to their clients. I began to realize, "Man, I've really created something powerful here." So I joined Coach2*, which was obviously an important step in terms of getting in a room with other people who are dealing with packaging issues. One initiative I've developed is a licensing program that we're rolling out over the next few months. We're going to hold training sessions and help other mortgage brokers become licensed in the 7 Steps process.

Dan Sullivan: *This process must be incredibly transformative for mortgage brokers and real estate agents. I mean, they're in a world where their life is totally dependent on interest rates and the sale of homes, and you've created a bypass around that.*
Philip Tirone: The freedom that mortgage brokers will receive from becoming licensed in the 7 Steps process is just staggering. I've experienced it. I mean, last year the lending market was down 20 to 30 percent, and we were up 20 percent.

Dan Sullivan: *You've also created a lot of additional platforms for getting 7 Steps out to consumers.*
Philip Tirone: We direct people to several places. They can go online and learn about our process at *www.7stepsto720.com*. If people want products, we've got books, workbooks, CDs, the whole package—all available on our website. If people want a more personalized level of assistance, we provide a private 30-minute coaching call for $499. We've also developed an 18-month coaching program, where we literally hold the client's

Our philosophy is that you don't need any gimmicks. Your credit score will improve over time if you simply follow the steps we've identified. It works all the time.

          *For the definition of Coach2, please see page 211.

hand—cross all the T's, dot all the I's—to make sure every step has been taken to get that person's credit where it needs to be. This program runs from $2,500 and up depending on the person's credit.

Dan Sullivan: *And you're also giving speeches.*
Philip Tirone: I've started attending conferences and giving speeches. I spoke at one conference in San Diego. There were 125 people in the audience, and 80 percent of those people either bought a book or CD, or signed up for the licensing program. So we had $22,000 in sales just at that event. Now, we're looking at doing infomercials.

Dan Sullivan: *How does that work?*
Philip Tirone: Basically, you can license a product to a company and get three percent royalties. Or you can hire a production company and fund all aspects of the production.

Dan Sullivan: *And you own it.*
Philip Tirone: Right. If you fund production yourself, the profits are more like 40 percent. You know, every time we've approached somebody about the non-licensing route, we ask them, "Would you like to forego your fee and get a piece of the pie?" I want to see how much they believe in the product. We've talked to four different people, and so far every single person has said, "We want a piece of the pie. We'll forego our fee." So that tells you something about the possible success of the infomercial.

Dan Sullivan: *I'm sure there are a lot of credit programs out there that don't really deliver. So I'd bet it's very reassuring for people to find a credit program that actually does what they expect it to do: raise credit scores.*
Philip Tirone: There are a lot of programs out there that say, "Pay us $1,000, and we'll get your credit score up." In reality, what's

happening is that the operator knows somebody at a finance company and uses his connections to get the client's credit score raised. But everything is dependent on that relationship with the finance company. 7 Steps to 720 uses a totally different approach. Our philosophy is that you don't need any gimmicks. Your credit score will improve over time if you simply follow the steps we've identified. It works all the time. That's why Nightingale-Conant chose us over other credit programs to be part of their network. When they looked at all the credit products, ours was the simplest, it made the most sense, and the results were predictable.

Dan Sullivan: *That consistency of results must be extraordinarily valuable to clients.*
Philip Tirone: Just recently, Dan, I had an experience that really demonstrates the kind of effect this is having on my business. A man was filing a loan application on a home whose purchase price was over $1 million. So we're talking about a $25,000 commission. This man was ready to give the business to another mortgage broker, but when the broker ran his credit score, he found it had dropped to 604. Basically, a lot of small mistakes, but that's what happens with credit. Anyway, his wife's score was 784. His real estate agent said, "You've got to call my friend, my main lender, Philip Tirone."

Dan Sullivan: *Another referral.*
Philip Tirone: Exactly. So the guy called me up, and I said, "Here's the thing. You're going into escrow. There's no way to raise your credit score this quickly. So we're going to need to do the loan in your wife's name." And they weren't surprised by that because it's really the advice any mortgage broker would give them. But then I was able to tell them, "By doing the loan with us, you'll get free enrollment in our 7 Steps credit repair program. It's an 18-month program that is going to basically guarantee that you'll get a 720 credit score the next time you

need to refinance." They called me the next morning and said, "We decided to use you."

Dan Sullivan: That's when you know you've got good intellectual capital. You're selling an experience that the person sees as crucial to their future, and they can't get it anywhere else.
Philip Tirone: I have to tell you, Dan, I'm burning with excitement right now just talking about this.

Dan Sullivan: That's the passion coming through.
Philip Tirone: The reason I'm so excited is because I know this is just the beginning. I mean, the loan business still represents 75 to 80 percent of my business. Last year, we did $1,750,000 in gross fees on loans. But the growth potential coming from 7 Steps—the growth potential coming from book sales, infomercials, licensing programs, credit coaching—is just enormous. As our process is unveiled on a national scale, I really believe that our revenue from these areas will surpass our revenue on the mortgage side.

Dan Sullivan: What's striking to me, Philip, is that your process really has the potential to impact millions of people and have an extraordinarily powerful effect on the economy as a whole.
Philip Tirone: Thanks, Dan. I feel the same way. Think about what would happen if we could get this in the hands of millions of people. President Bush gives a one-time $300 tax break, and that stimulates the economy. With my program, you're literally giving people a $6,000 to $7,000 tax break, because that's what they'll save through a higher credit score. The impact on the economy is just staggering. I like to think of it as the "credit score revolution."

Dan Sullivan: There are a lot of people who will become much more confident about their economic security. And we all know the importance of consumer confidence for a healthy economy.
Philip Tirone: Absolutely. With the credit system the way it

> *As a mortgage broker, I always tell real estate agents that I don't care if someone's been denied by other lenders, because I have a process that works.*

is, a lot of people feel that things are totally stacked against them. They're going to get beat up for failing. Interest rates are rising. Foreclosures are on the upswing. People come to me and say, "I had a bankruptcy three years ago. I need to become a cash-only citizen." And that's the totally wrong approach. People need to rebuild their credit as if they were eighteen years old. No matter how bad they've had it in the past, they can acquire a good credit score. As a mortgage broker, I always tell real estate agents that I don't care if someone's been denied by other lenders, because I have a process that works.

Dan Sullivan: *What has it meant for you, Philip, on a personal level, this total transformation of your business? You're a long way from Prescott, Arizona.*

Philip Tirone: It's hard to believe that only a few years ago, I was getting to work at 4:00 a.m. so I could dial 45,000 cold calls a year. It was an addiction. Now, I work hard, but I know how to refresh myself. I can delegate tasks to people around me. It may sound like a cliché, but the truth of the matter is that I'll never stop doing this. 7 Steps can have a huge impact on the world, but I'll never stop. Who knows what I'll create next?

By learning how to become an Industry Transformer, I feel like I'm running track in cleats while everyone else is barefoot. I have such a competitive advantage.

For contact details on 7 Steps to a 720 Credit Score, please see page 216.

INGREDIENT 6

Bypass

Ingredient 6

Bypass

One of the striking features of all the Unique Process entrepreneurs is that they seldom, if at all, talk about "the competition." They don't compare themselves to other entrepreneurs and companies in their industry, and they don't worry about them or try to copy them. In many ways, Unique Process entrepreneurs seem to operate and grow within their own custom-designed industries and marketplaces, free of all competitors.

David Allen expressed his view on this: *"We have more opportunities than we have capabilities, and the challenge is to be smart as we continue our dynamic growth. Sure, there are other companies; however, they are mostly mom-and-pop operations, and some of them do great and others don't. They are still struggling with The Ceiling of Complexity*, and we don't consider them to be our competition because they haven't created an identity or a strategy to reach the next level. Some of our competitors are wanting to become affiliated with our organization so we can teach them our Unique Process."*

David's attitude, which was repeated over and over in our interviews with the others in this book, points out another great advantage of the Unique Process approach: *bypass.* Within their Unique Process structures, and within their creative partnerships with clientele, these entrepreneurs are always bypassing anyone who attempts to compete with them.

*For the definition of The Ceiling of Complexity, please see page 211.

This is an enormous entrepreneurial freedom. Philip Tirone puts it this way: *"Most mortgage brokers talk about rates, and I believe people want to talk about their financial futures. As opposed to worrying about the rates my competitors offer, my time goes toward coming up with new ways to support my clients in getting their next home and attaining the lifestyle they dream about. My business is about people's dreams, and the confidence and capability they need to get there."*

The competition doesn't understand what is taking place. Many Unique Process entrepreneurs remark that even when they tell others in their industry what they are doing, and even how they are doing it, the response is usually non-comprehension, skepticism, disbelief, or even anger. Tony and Mary Miller, as part of their Dream Manager process, gave everyone in their company two extra paid weeks of vacation a year. They did this for a variety of reasons, but mainly so their employees would have a better quality of life and be more rejuvenated when they came to work.

Other janitorial companies in Cincinnati were incensed by this. Tony and Mary got angry phone calls and letters protesting against this "unfair strategy." The reason for the anger, of course, was that none of these other companies felt they could possibly implement this strategy. One of the results for Tony and Mary is that their staff turnover rate dropped from the usual industry average of 350 percent annually to 50 percent within the next 12 months. When you think about the impact on morale, work continuity, and lower expenses, it was a no-brainer, but none of the other companies followed their lead. With this one strategy as part of their Unique Process, Tony and Mary bypassed everyone else in their industry.

When you listen to Unique Process entrepreneurs, you get the sense that all of them operate in marketplaces of their own making. Because of how client and customer relationships are continually transformed inside of their processes, they get to spend most of their time and energy on creativity. Joe Polish says, *"I'm always on offense. I never play defense. I make everybody else play defense, all of the time."*

Characteristics of entrepreneurs who create bypasses.
In analyzing how these entrepreneurs continually grow and progress within their Unique Processes, I've noticed a number of factors that enable them to continually bypass their industries:

• They spend little time and energy involved with the "conventional" industry that they are in.

• They are oblivious to the "conventional wisdom" of how to be successful in their industry. They have their own custom-designed success formula that has less and less to do with what others are doing.

• They don't "hang out" with the established practitioners in their industry, those who represent the status quo. Instead, they search out and compare notes with "transformers" in other industries who are also creating bypasses.

• They continually innovate new concepts, strategies, systems, and methods that achieve results considered extraordinary by the standards of the industry.

• They attract a following of other entrepreneurs in their industry who are also looking for ways to bypass the conventional wisdom.

• Over time, because of their increased innovation and their following of like-minded entrepreneurs, these Unique Process entrepreneurs create an alternative "bypass industry" that is superior in obvious ways to the conventional one.

Our experience is that all entrepreneurs who commit them-selves to a Unique Process create strategies and methods that bypass the conventions of their industry. As they continue to do this, they increasingly operate in their own competition-free marketplace with excited staff, enthusiastic and appreciative clients, and admiring followers. But sometimes they are so successful at doing this that they attract large companies who either try to buy them out or steal everything they have created.

Don Munce tells the story of a "competitor" who tries to copy everything that he produces. Don's response to this is to innovate entirely new value offerings and solutions that make everything he did the previous year obsolete. But that's just a small part of the success story featured in our next interview. Don's Unique Process not only enables him to continually bypass the competition, but to transform how more than a million high school graduates every year find the right colleges and universities. On the other side of the coin, he shows thou-sands of colleges and universities how to attract the students that will do best at their institutions.

Don Munce

Creating A Brighter Future
For America's Youth

Don Munce was always entrepreneurial, but for over a decade worked in an institutional setting in college admissions. Recruited to work for the company he now owns, Missouri-based National Research Center for College & University Admissions™ (NRCCUA), Don soon designed and implemented a Unique Process that took advantage of constant technological advances and focused on strengthening relationships in the education community. As a result, he has become the untouchable leader in the $10-billion industry that helps students and colleges find their best possible match.

Dan Sullivan: *To begin, Don, why don't we talk a bit about how your entrepreneurial career got started?*
Don Munce: Well, my mother was a bookkeeper, and from an early age, she encouraged me to be an entrepreneur. I think I'm one of several people in the Coach program who started off running things like paper routes, and that was certainly a valuable experience at a young age. During high school and college, I ran my own fireworks stand. Then, I started working as Director of Admissions at a small college in Kansas, but on the side, I hired a bunch of college kids to open a sandwich shop. So I guess I've always been involved in some sort of entrepreneurial venture without really consciously thinking about it. It has just always seemed like the natural thing to do.

Dan Sullivan: *But you also had some early experience actually working for colleges.*
Don Munce: That's right. I spent 12 years working in college admissions. Then in 1987, I was recruited from the college ranks to serve as director of sales for the company I now own. After only 11 months, this organization was facing bankruptcy, because the owner had taken out loans he couldn't repay.

Having four children and having lived in Kansas City less than a year, my choice was to either go work for someone else, or find a creative way to eliminate the financial burden on this company.

Dan Sullivan: *Your entrepreneurial instincts kicked in.*
Don Munce: Exactly, but it was a tough challenge. We're talking about almost a million dollars in debt that I had to find a way to pay off. At that time, I was only making about $40,000 a year, driving an Oldsmobile station wagon, and renting a house. So where in the world was I going to find a million dollars? I started networking, and eventually I found an individual in Chicago who was willing to invest and execute a loan that I assured him I'd pay off, even if it took 25 years. It only took two and a half years to repay nearly the entire loan, and the company has been moving forward ever since.

Dan Sullivan: *How exciting.*
Don Munce: It was very exciting, and, of course, a little scary, but a lot of great things happened in the process.

Dan Sullivan: *Just for the sake of readers, can you provide a little background on the sort of problems that your company solves in the educational marketplace?*
Don Munce: My company is called the National Research Center for College & University Admissions (NRCCUA). And we've found that colleges and universities—both traditional non-profit institutions and for-profit career colleges—all have the same basic problem: They need to efficiently identify students that might eventually want to enroll, and they need to market to those students by opening up a dialogue.

Dan Sullivan: *Could you give an example?*
Don Munce: Sure. If you're the director of admissions at a small Baptist college in Iowa with about 800 students and ten

career offerings, and there are 40 small private colleges like that in the state of Iowa, your challenge is to find the needle in the haystack. You want to find the students in Iowa or in surrounding states who might be interested in attending a Baptist college as opposed to a large state university, because they want to be involved in that particular type of atmosphere. Many of the small non-profit colleges we work with are operating on a limited budget. They don't have seasoned staff in the area of marketing and sales. So we provide enormous value.

Dan Sullivan: Isn't it the case that many people in these academic institutions remain averse to anything that looks like sales and marketing?

Don Munce: Absolutely. It remains a big issue for us from a public relations standpoint. There's a presumption that colleges are doing too much marketing and putting too much pressure on kids. But we see our role as a positive one—helping both students and colleges find the best possible match.

Dan Sullivan: Don, why don't you talk about the growth of your company and the different services you offer, because I know they're quite extensive?

Don Munce: Well, our company was actually founded in the 1960s. The original founder had the idea to create a survey and distribute it through guidance counselors to high school students, who could indicate their preferences. When I took over the company, I immediately went to some colleagues of mine who were experienced admissions officers and brought them in as co-workers. The level of service and experience immediately took a jump. You know, our biggest competition is the testing agencies. When students take the ACT, for example, they have an opportunity to check a box and have their information sent to colleges and universities. But we immediately started adding services that far surpassed what colleges were getting from the testing agencies.

Dan Sullivan: *How many years ago are we talking?*

Don Munce: This was about 18 years ago. At that time, we already had records on a few million students, and we had a hundred different pieces of information about those students. For example, if you were the admissions officer at a Jewish institution in Los Angeles, and all you did as an institution was train rabbis, you could go into our database and request the names of young people who were interested in attending a Jewish institution and who were also interested in studying theology or religion. Now, at the time, we had these giant printouts of paper that we had to go through, and it took about two or three hours before we could come back to the college and say, "Here are the 1,142 students that meet your criteria." Then we would place an order through a processing center, and in a few weeks we could get them the precise information.

Dan Sullivan: *You needed a technological breakthrough to speed up the process.*

Don Munce: Exactly. I was able to find a computer guy in Kansas City who figured out how to manage our database so that when we were on the phone talking to colleges, we could pull up all of the information instantaneously. That change caused our sales to skyrocket, because colleges were much more motivated to place orders. Through the years, we've really been at the forefront of helping colleges take advantage of technology. For example, we were the first organization to actually start collecting email addresses and providing those email addresses to colleges so they could add that information to their communication stream.

Dan Sullivan: *Don, as we sit here in 2008, how many students are in your database?*

Don Munce: Eighteen years ago we worked with about 200 colleges. Now, we work with 2,200 colleges on an annual basis and we have almost six million students in our database. At any one time, there are about 12 million high school students in the United States, so we're approaching 50 percent of the total student body.

Dan Sullivan: Wow. It's great to hear those numbers, Don. You know, I remember that you went through a real crossover in terms of understanding what your company could actually do. When did you start realizing that the entire operation was actually a Unique Process?

Don Munce: I think one of the major turning points was when I started to confront the 300-pound gorilla in college admissions, which is the College Board. When I took over NRCCUA®, around 70 percent of four-year colleges and universities in the country were using them as their only source of information about kids. NRCCUA's market share was about three percent. Then it occurred to me: I wonder how many of the students I'm surveying have not yet taken a College Board test? So I started talking to colleges that weren't previously interested in our service because they thought they were getting all the information from the College Board. Basically, I told them that if they ordered from us, we'd deduplicate any students that were already in the College Board database. Meanwhile, they'd have access to many students who weren't in their database.

Dan Sullivan: You minimized their risk.
Don Munce: Absolutely. And overnight, this process switch created massive amounts of new business. It put us in an entirely different position against the 300-pound gorilla.

Dan Sullivan: What's interesting, Don, is that you've continued to improve the process. Could you talk about some of your latest innovations in the area of right-fit matching?
Don Munce: Sure. We're very excited about a new project

*The relationships that we've cultivated in
the education community are the reason our
process can't be copied.*

that has grown out of ideas I generated in Coach2®. It's a new
service called mycollegeoptions.com. This is a counseling site
that allows students to go on and fill out a questionnaire indi-
cating the kinds of things they're interested in when it comes to
their college experience. Then they receive an instant five-star
matching report that identifies the colleges most closely aligned
with their goals and aspirations.

*Dan Sullivan: You're making the students active participants
in the information-gathering process.*
Don Munce: Exactly. When their attitudes change, students
can go in and create a new match report. They'll be able to
create their own custom college planning profile. And then,
every time a college or university comes to us and accesses
the name of this student, we'll be able to notify the student
that a particular school has just asked for information. So what
we're creating is an interactive space where colleges are going
to have branding and recognition opportunities on a real-time
basis with students as they go through the planning process.

*Dan Sullivan: Don, how has your competition responded to all
these innovations that have developed over the years?*
Don Munce: We have one direct competitor. He was a high-
ranking official at one of our vendors, who left his employer
on unpleasant terms. After a couple years of non-compete,
he decided to take the business secrets that he knew about
NRCCUA and create a survey process to mimic what we were
doing. I actually have documents going back to 1999 showing

that every single year, we came out with new direct mail to go to high schools. The next year this guy had almost identical stuff. So as a business, we know that every year we have to innovate.

Dan Sullivan: *What a great benefit he has been to you.*
Don Munce: He's caused me to do a lot of things I never would have done. We now work with about 20 different research partners. These are professional teacher organizations and community-based organizations, who are surveying their member teachers and the students of their member teachers on our behalf. The relationships that we've cultivated in the education community are the reason our process can't be copied.

Dan Sullivan: *Don, from the vantage point of almost 20 years with the company, where do you see the future of this industry as it goes forward? You've created an enormous amount of intellectual capital. What are the major growth opportunities, because I've got to believe that higher education in the United States is a constantly changing industry?*
Don Munce: This is actually about a $10-billion industry—that's how much colleges and universities spend on an annual basis to identify and recruit their freshman class. They hire admission staff. They buy lists. They do direct mail. They advertise in magazines. And altogether, it's a $10 billion effort. Institutions need vehicles like NRCCUA to drive this recruitment process, so we're really at the center of the process. From our perspective, the student database is only the starting point.

Dan Sullivan: *I understand that you were considering a sale about 18 months ago but didn't go through with it. What was your thinking on that?*
Don Munce: I thought I knew everything about the acquisition process before I went through it myself. But the truth is that you really are going to kindergarten when you jump into a situation

where you've got a large company interested in acquiring your company. It's very flattering, especially when a lot of big numbers are thrown around, and you start thinking about what you could accomplish in the next phase of your life with those numbers. They wanted to keep me on, so of course I had a lot of questions about my ability to control the staff and make decisions relating to the future growth of the company. What happened was over the last 48 hours before closing, some issues came up that from my end I thought I could live with, but from their end they just really could not live through. For example, I was quite reluctant to agree to the company's executive vacation plan.

Dan Sullivan: *Don, I can't tell you how many deals there are where the deal breaker is control of your personal time. The truth is they didn't want you taking too much more than four weeks.*
Don Munce: Yeah. Unfortunately, as I negotiated this deal over the course of a year, I got a bit disconnected from the future of my company. So when the deal fell through, it was really painful for a few days. Then I woke up one day and looked at my wife, Marie, and said, "I'm so relieved. This gives me my life back, and now I can start thinking about the future."

Dan Sullivan: *So you had a near-death experience.*
Don Munce: That's a really good way to describe it. Now, over the course of the last year, we've had a lot of exciting developments. One of my sons has come into the business. He's very entrepreneurial, and he's got real strengths working with website technologies, so we're exploring a lot of new opportunities.

Before, nobody did what we do in such a comprehensive, systematic way. Matching the right student with the right college is what we're all about.

Dan Sullivan: *From an industry transformation standpoint, Don, if you were to pinpoint one or two innovations that really changed the way people look at the link-up between colleges and students, what would they be?*

Don Munce: I think one key innovation was when NRCCUA took the lead years ago in bringing in a lot of seasoned admissions people. You know, when compared to the college testing companies, NRCCUA is in the unique position of focusing all of our attention on this issue. That's all we do. We don't do 45 other things. It's come to the point where even people at other organizations are trying to be more like us when they approach colleges and universities. We've really evolved into the leader in what we do.

Dan Sullivan: *You essentially created the industry.*

Don Munce: We've created it. Before, nobody did what we do in such a comprehensive, systematic way. Matching the right student with the right college is what we're all about. Organizations like the testing companies can't do it. They don't have the relationships. They don't have the people. They don't know how to get the people and train the people. So now we're dead even with College Board and double the market share of ACT, and that's after starting out at three percent 20 years ago.

Dan Sullivan: *What's striking to me, Don, is that we're talking about potentially millions of students who may not have found the right college without your programs.*

Don Munce: One expert outside of our company has indicated that about 20 percent of the annual enrollment at four-year private colleges across the country wouldn't be there without the NRCCUA connection. In some cases it's much higher than 20 percent. So that's pretty phenomenal. You know, many of the entrepreneurs in Strategic Coach have

I wake up every day thankful that I have a chance to go make a difference doing something I love doing.

children who've experienced the college recruitment process. They see this mail coming, and they don't know the story behind it. When I travel and meet other entrepreneurs, it only takes a few minutes for them to understand that somebody's got to figure out how to identify their child instead of the kid down the street. So we've touched countless families.

Dan Sullivan: Don, what has this meant for you, this 20-year journey?

Don Munce: I wake up every day thankful that I have a chance to go make a difference doing something I love doing. As a young man growing up in South Dakota, looking at Mount Rushmore and thinking about the guy who carved it, I really hoped that someday in my life I'd have a chance to make a big difference. I've seen a lot of those dreams come true, and the journey isn't even close to being over.

For contact details on Creating A Brighter Future For America's Youth, please see page 215.

Intellectual Capital

Intellectual Capital

The factor that most differentiates Unique Process entrepreneurs from all others is the continual creation and proprietary ownership of intellectual capital. Don Munce explains it this way: *"When I first got into business, I paid to use other people's ideas and tools. Now we create our own, and other people pay us to use them."*

Like everyone else or uniquely different and famous.
The vast majority of entrepreneurs spend their entire careers using and selling other people's tools. Joe Polish has a useful metaphor to describe how most business people operate:

"It's like selling hamburgers. It's not your recipe, and they aren't your ingredients. It doesn't even matter how you serve them, they're still burgers, not much different from the ones next door. Nobody's going to pay you for the recipe, or for your business when you get out. Most entrepreneurs are running hamburger stands that are like thousands of others. On the other hand, there are great chefs who charge $500 per person to eat a meal at their restaurant. They have a three-month waiting list to get in. Every night they have a different menu, which is uniquely theirs. The best cooks and waiters want to work for them. The famous and powerful want to eat there. Not only that, they publish cookbooks filled with their recipes, and sell tens of thousands of them at $50 a book. And they have television shows that are syndicated around

the world. Their market value is in the tens of millions. They have thousands of loyal customers, and tens of thousands of admiring fans. A few entrepreneurs are like that, and I aim to be one of them."

Creativity, packaging, reputation, and ownership.
Following up on Joe's observation, the difference between a burger stand and a five-star restaurant, then, is intellectual capital. The difference is in the creativity, in the packaging, in the reputation, and in the ownership.

As a coach for more than 30 years, I've found that most successful entrepreneurs have creative ideas that they use in day-to-day business, but they never go any further than that. They never create anything that effectively differentiates them. They may be great at what they do, but it's not immediately obvious. When they die or retire, their creativity goes with them. Nobody remembers who they were, or what they did.

Unique Process entrepreneurs are very different. They go a crucial step further, capturing their ideas and packaging them so that many other people can use them. Once they are in packaged form, everybody knows where the ideas came from.

Philip Tirone reports that people all over America now know who he is, and about his ideas, since he packaged them as a Unique Process, 7 Steps to a 720 Credit Score: *"As a mortgage broker, I only met clients who needed to buy homes in Los Angeles; however, since I packaged 7 Steps to a 720 Credit Score into a Unique Process, my world is changing. I'm being asked to be the guest speaker at conferences; I'm having my competition buy my process from me in order to grow their business. Mortgage brokers, financial advisors, and real estate agents have all gone through our licensing program as a way to distinguish themselves from their competition and add more value to their clients, which instantly breaks them out of the Commoditization Trap. This is all possible because of Coach2; prior to Coach2, I simply had a self-published book. I did not, however, have the understanding of intellectual capital like I do now. I'm excited to see the impact 7 Steps will have on our economy in the years to come!"*

Your ideas multiplied many times over in other brains.
The difference that intellectual capital makes in an entrepreneur's life starts with the packaging. It can be in written form, it can be in the form of graphics or diagrams, or be transformed into software or multimedia presentations. But the bottom line is that it is always a much better idea—and every marketplace loves better ideas. Whatever form it takes, the result of intellectual capital is that the power of your ideas gets multiplied in other people's minds. Your ideas have your stamp on them, but they can be extraordinarily useful to many other people who don't need you to be there to help them.

People love to buy the recipe books by famous chefs. They don't reproduce the same great meals exactly, but if they follow the instructions, the meal is usually a lot better than what they would have come up with on their own. And they're a lot more confident about having another dinner party.

Unique Process entrepreneurs use their packaged ideas—their intellectual capital—to create great teams and enterprises. David Allen says that he would never have been able to create a global company without the packaged ideas that are in his Unique Process.

Mary and Tony Miller have just signed a licensing agreement whose annual fees will exceed the net revenues of their janitorial company. Tony is very excited: *"Our intellectual capital is incredibly more profitable than our main janitorial business. We're going to get million-dollar checks every year for just a single one of the technical processes that we've packaged. We have few, if any, expenses with this transaction. All they want is our process—our packaged creativity. The licensee is a multi-billion-dollar corporation. They have all the infra-structure and a big market share. What they are lacking is the new intellectual capital that makes their infrastructure more productive and profitable. For that they are eager to write mil-lion-dollar checks."*

The best of all entrepreneurial worlds.

Increasingly, Unique Process entrepreneurs use their pack-aged wisdom and creativity to differentiate themselves in their marketplaces, and to bypass the limitations and restrictions of their industries. The excitement that arises from the activity of creating intellectual capital, and the increased wealth creation that comes with it, keeps these individuals continually reju-venated as business people. Once they start down this road, you never hear any Unique Process entrepreneur talking about retirement or about selling their company. Their packaged cre-ativity puts them in the best of all entrepreneurial worlds. They have freedom over their time, over their money, over their relationships, and over their lifetime purpose. What could be better? Why would they ever want to stop doing this?

Gary Boomer, featured in our next interview, feels that he lives in an ideal entrepreneurial world. It's in accounting. Let's see how Gary is transforming this industry with a combination of creativity and cooperation.

Gary Boomer
The Boomer Technology Circles™

Gary Boomer's early experience at one of the Big Eight accounting firms gave him a solid background in the profession. But it was his love of technology and its ability to increase efficiency in the accounting industry that intrigued him. As a consultant, he created The Boomer Technology Circles™, a Unique Process that not only, responds to the future of the accounting firm in a world of swift technological change, but that addresses myriad key issues and strategic planning challenges in the accounting industry.

Dan Sullivan: Let's begin, Gary, by talking about your history in the accounting industry. Where did you begin, and then what was it like when you started going out there with an approach much different from what people were used to in the conventional sense?

Gary Boomer: Well, I graduated with a bachelor's degree in accounting, and I started off with one of the Big Eight accounting firms, which happened to be located in Kansas City. Then, I got a masters degree in accounting and went to work at a small firm in Manhattan, Kansas, where I still have a residence today. Over the next 20 years, this small firm grew into a regional accounting firm with two offices and over 50 people. But I eventually began to feel limited, and after joining the Strategic Coach Program, it became clear that I was having a really difficult time utilizing my Unique Ability. I was an entrepreneur at heart, but I was operating in an environment that didn't allow for much entrepreneurship.

Dan Sullivan: What bothered you the most?

Gary Boomer: Basically, most of the people in my accounting firm were focused on time and effort rather than results. Yet my entrepreneurial spirit led me to resist this outlook. It came to the point where I couldn't, and didn't want to, work any more hours in this kind of environment.

Dan Sullivan: *At what stage did you finally leave the accounting firm and go independent?*
Gary Boomer: I left the firm in my second year of the Coach program, and it has now been about 11 years since I left public accounting. However, I had already started my con-sulting practice within the accounting firm, so it was now just a matter of allowing that consulting practice to reach its full potential.

Dan Sullivan: *Nowhere here have I heard that you love bal-ancing accounts and doing ledger sheets.*
Gary Boomer: Exactly. I always considered that boring and repetitive work. In contrast, I have always been interested in how technology can be used as an accelerator within the accounting industry. Of course, in an industry that bills by the hour, there's the concern that if technology makes you more efficient and reduces hours, it also might reduce client revenue.

Dan Sullivan: *In other words, a real bypass is required, not just from an operational standpoint, but from a thinking standpoint.*
Gary Boomer: Absolutely. And I think many people in the profession today are caught because they don't know how to escape. They have a pretty comfortable lifestyle. They make good money. They're respected in the community. But they don't know how to break out and develop something that's more meaningful and more valuable.

Dan Sullivan: *What happens to accounting firms when they're conflicted like that?*
Gary Boomer: It causes a lot of internal strife within the firm

since so many partners are going in different directions. Rather than being a vision-based partnership, the firm basically becomes a service company.

Dan Sullivan: *The partners are essentially just sharing expenses.*
Gary Boomer: Yes. They aren't really entrepreneurs; they're just professionals sharing overhead.

Dan Sullivan: *Gary, when you began doing consulting work, when did you start noticing that you could have a really powerful impact on the industry?*
Gary Boomer: First of all, when the personal computer came out, it immediately transformed the industry. You know, I remember in the mid-1980s, there was still a lot of boiler-plate work that accountants were charging out at fairly high prices. The PC meant that you no longer had to run 10-key adding machines to determine if the totals were correct.

Dan Sullivan: *But you found that even as technology developed, the firms weren't necessarily using it effectively.*
Gary Boomer: They were trying to incorporate a lot of fancy technology, but it was basically being used as a 2-GigaHertz typewriter. They still had the same processes that were in place 15 to 20 years ago.

Dan Sullivan: *So at this point, Gary, you set out to develop your own independent practice, Boomer Consulting, to help firms with their technology needs. What kind of organization were you looking to create?*
Gary Boomer: It's interesting because when I left the accounting firm, five people in my department decided to go with me. Today, I still have two of those people. One woman started out as a strategic assistant, and she's since become one

Our goal has always been to function as a kind of mediator between the technologists and the business people. When accounting firms feel confident about technology, they'll invest in the right technology and hire the right people.

of our top consultants. Her name is Sandra Wiley, and she's just been a huge contributor. There are several other people I could talk about. You know, our goal has never been to employ the world, but to try and transform the accounting industry. Today, we have 13 people and we're much closer to transformation than we were ten years ago, that's for sure.

Dan Sullivan: Great. Let's talk a little more about that transformation agenda. If we could recreate the conversations you were having with accounting firms ten years ago, how did those conversations sound?
Gary Boomer: Our first question was something along the lines of, "What kind of return are you getting on your investment in technology?"

Dan Sullivan: And the firms didn't even know what you were talking about.
Gary Boomer: Right. Our second question was, "How much are you spending on technology?"

Dan Sullivan: And they probably didn't know how to answer that question either.
Gary Boomer: They always had one of two responses: Either we're spending too much, or spending too little. We came up with a methodology to really help them get clear about their investment in technology. Let's suppose a firm was paying

somebody $5 an hour to work on client issues. They'd probably bill that client between $15 and $20 an hour for the work. So my basic message was, "Why don't you do the same for technology? If technology is reducing the number of hours you need to devote to clients, then why don't you find a way to get compensated for that?"

Dan Sullivan: *So you developed a technology surcharge.*
Gary Boomer: That's right. If a firm charged $100 an hour, they would basically add on another $15 for technology. Many firms were reluctant, but they tried it, and, sure enough, they got very little resistance from the clients. Most clients are actually relieved that the firm is being proactive about technology because they know it saves hours and makes the work more efficient.

Dan Sullivan: *And, of course, you developed a lot of other more specific strategies to help firms utilize particular technologies.*
Gary Boomer: Exactly. You know, there's often a big gap between entrepreneurs and technologists. Our goal has always been to function as a kind of mediator between the technologists and the business people. When accounting firms feel confident about technology, they'll invest in the right technology and hire the right people.

Dan Sullivan: *What you're doing is actually, for the first time, giving the technologist a proper role at the very center of the profit-making structure of the firm.*
Gary Boomer: We're encouraging firms to put their top technology person at the CIO or executive level so they're familiar with the company's strategy, and the other executives are familiar with technology's role in executing that strategy.

Dan Sullivan: *In other words, your consulting efforts started to move beyond technology into more general strategy issues.*
Gary Boomer: Absolutely. We learned that in many companies, the technology is actually better than the strategic plan. So we developed a comprehensive method for strategic planning, and we now make more money from strategic planning than from technology planning.

Dan Sullivan: *Now, in the first few years, you were consulting on a one-on-one basis for individual clients. At what point did you start putting firms into circles with one another?*
Gary Boomer: Well, the demand was coming from our clients. They wanted a place where they could get coaching, but also learn from other participants. I tried to pattern the program on the model you've used so successfully at Strategic Coach, and also the Quality Dealer Circles in the automobile industry. Basically, I realized that if I could get people to come to me in larger multiples, all at once, we could expand significantly. So we developed The Boomer Technology Circles. Each circle comprises about 20 to 25 comparably sized firms representing different geographic regions. We require that both the firm's technology person and its decision maker come as a team, and everyone has to pay upfront.

Dan Sullivan: *Why don't you talk a bit about the format of these meetings?*
Gary Boomer: Sure. Our meetings last a day and a half because we want to create some networking opportunities. People usually come in on Sunday evening and leave at noon on Tuesday. On Monday, we start with a session on strategy and vision, where I talk about some of the latest trends in the industry and how it impacts them. Then we break into groups of five and have what we call The Accountability Review.

Basically, at each session, participants build a 90-day game plan, and The Accountability Review allows them to reflect on the progress that has occurred since their previous session. We give everybody a copy of the gameplan that they developed 90 days ago, and then they share with the group what's been accomplished and what hasn't been accomplished. It's a great motivator when firms know they're going to be exposed to peer pressure every 90 days.

Dan Sullivan: *What other activities occur?*
Gary Boomer: We offer a variety of sessions focused on IT strategy. We also offer service reviews of new technology products, along with access to leading industry vendors.

Dan Sullivan: *What kinds of reactions do the participants have when they complete these sessions?*
Gary Boomer: The sessions build their confidence by allowing them to see what other firms are doing. When five other firms in that circle can share their experiences, it cuts down the research and development time by multiples.

Dan Sullivan: *Are there any stories you can share with us, Gary, in terms of a particular firm that just took off like a rocket when they started going through this?*
Gary Boomer: I remember one firm out of New Jersey. They were struggling with whether to implement technology internally or outsource that technology. After going through our planning processes, they eventually made the business decision to outsource most of their technology, even while retaining a few internal people. They're now in a position to take their technology from one office and replicate it in another office because it's all online. This approach has allowed them to grow throughout the Northeast and become a major player in the New York/New Jersey market.

Dan Sullivan: *How long does that sort of transformation take?*
Gary Boomer: Usually about five years. And we've seen major changes in only two years.

Dan Sullivan: *Gary, the common image of accountants is that they are kind of dry and dull. But I have a feeling that the experience of joining a Boomer Technology Circle really brings out a high degree of emotion in the participants.*
Gary Boomer: Absolutely. There's that stereotypical image that many accountants probably deserve, but it only goes so far. Regardless, we're talking about some of the most trusted advisors for business people, and I don't know any other group of professionals that's more trustworthy or sincere about what they're trying to do for their clients.

Dan Sullivan: *Gary, could you talk about the kinds of firms that are in the best position to benefit from The Boomer Technology Circles?*
Gary Boomer: Sure. Our program isn't for everyone. If a firm doesn't believe in some of the values we believe in, if it isn't client focused, and if it isn't committed to learning, then it could be a disruptive force in our program. But most firms self-select and do their research before coming into the program, especially because we require a significant upfront financial commitment. In terms of revenue, we usually work with firms who have revenue above $5 million. But a niche market firm who has revenue around $1 to $2 million can also be a very attractive client if they have the right kind of people in leadership positions.

Dan Sullivan: *Let's talk about numbers, Gary. You started your first Circle when? And how many Circles do you have now?*
Gary Boomer: We started our first in 2000, and we now have seven.

Dan Sullivan: *So while you started off working with maybe three or four firms, you're now up to 120 to 150 firms.*
Gary Boomer: That's correct.

Dan Sullivan: *In terms of overall growth, if I compare ten years ago with today, what are we talking about?*
Gary Boomer: My personal production is probably up by a factor of three at least. But that's only the beginning. The next big wave is coming because we've not only created the Circle community, we've created two other pieces of intellectual capital: The Performance$^{3\text{TM}}$ Formula and The Boomer Knowledge Network.

Dan Sullivan: *Great. Let's hear more.*
Gary Boomer: Well, The Boomer Knowledge Network is an online community that brings together industry leaders. We've set it up on a pay-subscription basis. It really provides a great forum for firms to collaborate with each other around issues like technology management, talent retention, and wider strategic planning challenges. It's particularly useful for firms that are already members of a Boomer Technology Circle and want to interact between meetings.

Dan Sullivan: *What kind of content do you offer?*
Gary Boomer: The online Knowledge Network includes multimedia features like videos and podcasts that provide expert overview of the industry's most pressing issues. It includes management metrics. It includes a variety of articles contributed by consultants, industry experts, and fellow community members. And the site also features downloadable tools that are quite useful to subscribers.

Dan Sullivan: *What about The Boomer Advantage Guides™?*

> *Our basic philosophy is that planning
> times people times processes equals performance,
> with technology being the accelerator.*

Gary Boomer: I'm glad you asked about that. The Boomer Advantage Guides are an approach we've developed to package the intellectual capital that we've accumulated over many years in the industry. Each guide goes in-depth on an important issue facing the industry, and we publish a new guide each quarter. The guides are printed in paper form and are also available electronically to all subscribers of the Boomer Knowledge Network.

Dan Sullivan: Huge for positioning.
Gary Boomer: I like to think of them as the CliffsNotes of the industry. If a client has a particular problem, we have a guide to address that.

Dan Sullivan: Let's talk about The Performance^3 Formula.
Gary Boomer: Sure thing. The Performance^3 Formula is a consulting formula we developed to help firms make more money, attract quality people, and grow their business. Our basic philosophy is that planning times people times processes equals performance, with technology being the accelerator. So we help firms in each of those areas. We help them develop a strategic plan, and nurture the right people, while making sure their processes support that plan.

Dan Sullivan: It's basically become a comprehensive platform for your consulting services.
Gary Boomer: That's right. And we've also developed The

Performance^{3}™ Management Program™, which is designed specifically for firm managers. This program really integrates all of our insights and applies them in the area of management skills. It's a two-year program with bi-yearly sessions, and each session is followed up with a private coaching call.

Dan Sullivan: *I understand that your son, Jim Boomer, has become heavily involved in this program.*

Gary Boomer: Both Jim Boomer and Sandra Wiley are leading the Performance^{3} Management initiative. They are doing it under the umbrella of Boomer Consulting, but it's really the Jim Boomer and Sandra Wiley show. Jim has been with Arthur Andersen and BearingPoint, so he has a real familiarity with the accounting industry and the technology issues we deal with. But Jim also has an MBA from the University of Texas, making him very comfortable with the wider management issues. Jim has a skill set that I don't have, so he's incredibly valuable. I also have to give Sandra Wiley a lot of credit. Sandra is not only great with our clients, but great in terms of human resource and human capital issues within our firm.

Dan Sullivan: *Hiring has probably become a lot easier.*

Gary Boomer: Exactly. We're putting a fantastic team together that allows me to operate within my Unique Ability. Hiring the right people had been a challenge up until the last five years. Now, we seem to hit every time we hire.

Dan Sullivan: *Do you see the firm getting much larger?*

Gary Boomer: Not significantly. We might have 20 people one day. That's only a few more employees than we have right now, but I also see us growing five to ten times larger in revenue.

Dan Sullivan: *And that's because of the intellectual capital.*

Gary Boomer: Right. That was a leap of faith. I knew I could make a good living doing one-on-one consulting, and maybe a Circle or two. Our expansion has required significant investment, but the investment has been well worthwhile, no question about it.

Dan Sullivan: *Let's talk about the competitive advantage of the firms you work with. How much better are they positioned in the marketplace as a result of what you're doing with them?*
Gary Boomer: It all starts with D.O.S.* All of our guides, all of our consulting services, are constructed around client D.O.S.™ So that's where the benefits come. For example, last year, one of the dangers that clients told us about was a need to upgrade their client list. They only have so many hours to sell, so they need to filter their lower-level clients. We came up with a filtering mechanism that many of the firms now use. So that's a typical example.

Dan Sullivan: *If you didn't exist, what would happen to these firms?*
Gary Boomer: They would go to a variety of different sources, none of whom could pull everything together. They would go to one guy for strategic planning, one guy for technology, one guy for education programs.

Dan Sullivan: *They wouldn't have the cross-fertilization, and they wouldn't have the community.*
Gary Boomer: Right. Our job is to keep confidence up. These firms are competitive so when they see their peers, they think, "If you can do that, we can do that."

■ *... some of the biggest organizations out there are coming to us interested in our intellectual capital.* ■

*For the definition of D.O.S., please see page 211.

Dan Sullivan: *Gary, if you could just stand back for a moment and think about how the industry looks at Gary Boomer and Boomer Consulting, what would their impression be?*
Gary Boomer: I think the industry is really impressed by the way we've reinvented our company, and they probably think we're a lot bigger organization than we actually are, because our capabilities have increased so dramatically.

Dan Sullivan: *It's interesting to hear you say that, Gary. You know, when we line up all eight of the Industry Transformers that are being featured in this book, the one thing that comes out is that these entrepreneurs are projecting an image in the marketplace that's way, way larger than the number of people actually working for them. How would you explain that impact?*
Gary Boomer: Over the years, we've been very willing to document and share our intellectual property. Once we learned the difference between intellectual property and intellectual capital, we started leveraging that property into capital. When people look at us, they say your size doesn't matter. You guys have the best content. You guys have the best ideas and the best processes.

Dan Sullivan: *Do you have any imitators?*
Gary Boomer: Sure we do, but none of them are willing to make the investment in people and process. They set up a one-man shop and try to use our stuff, but nobody has been able to do what we're doing in the marketplace.

Dan Sullivan: *Gary, let's look ahead ten years. What's next? What does the future look like from your perspective?*
Gary Boomer: One of our visions is to open this material up to individual accountants as opposed to firms. Even if the leader of a firm doesn't want to be involved, individual accountants can join our online communities using money out of their own

pocket. On the other end of the spectrum, some of the biggest organizations out there are coming to us interested in our intellectual capital. Next week I'm going to be meeting with the Big Four and some of the firms right below them in size. I don't think they would have called the meeting if we didn't have something of interest to them. They want to know how our processes might help them deal with some of their own internal problems.

Dan Sullivan: We're talking about thousands and thousands of individuals in these large firms. If you were given the opportunity to go in and make a substantial impact, where would your initial focus be?

Gary Boomer: First, they have to determine what their vision is and where they're headed, and communicate that vision to thousands of employees. At the same time, they have to show those employees why they are significant to the future of the company. Right now, these firms are losing many people after three years. Employees get good basic training when they go in, but there often isn't a good structure for professional development. So that's an issue that needs to be addressed.

Dan Sullivan: Gary, if thousands more firms were using the Boomer approach and Boomer technology, what would it do to the accounting industry worldwide?

Gary Boomer: These firms wouldn't have the personnel problems they have today because more people would want to go into the industry. People would view it as a much more exciting industry than it is perceived today.

Dan Sullivan: What about the impact on clients?

Gary Boomer: Clients would get much better service, more innovative service—and relationships would become much more important.

Dan Sullivan: *And what about profitability for the firms?*

Gary Boomer: The firms would be tremendously more profitable because they wouldn't have the turnover problems and they'd be in a position to offer services that are value-based, not hourly-based.

Dan Sullivan: *That's the big transition, isn't it?*

Gary Boomer: Right. They have to understand commoditization in order to get out of it.

Dan Sullivan: *It's been wonderful to hear your story, Gary. What have you taken from this interview? You're always learning, so I wonder what you've learned by going through this interview?*

Gary Boomer: I think gratitude is the first word that comes to mind: gratitude for my team at Boomer Consulting, and gratitude for Strategic Coach for allowing me to reach this position. It's been, what, 12 or 13 years since I've known you, and it gets better all the time. I was one of the first participants in Coach2, and what's great is that I really feel there's a support network in Coach2, a sounding board of people that speak the same language. The other big word is excitement. When I tell this story, I can't help but focus on the opportunities and rewards that are going to come my way over the next 25 years. The future really is brighter.

For contact details on The Boomer Technology Circles, please see page 213.

Monopoly

Monopoly

Deep in their competitive hearts, all entrepreneurs want their own marketplace monopoly. On the surface they may say they love competition, but I don't believe it. I've discovered from decades of discussions with thousands of entrepreneurs that what they really love is being more in control of their personal and professional futures. In Strategic Coach, Unique Process entrepreneurs achieve what we call "value creation monopolies," which provide that sense of control.

Permanent and practical ownership of a market niche.
Richard Rossi frequently talks about what a pleasure it is to spend most of his time imagining and talking about a bigger future for his company. The reason he is free to do this is that he and Barbara Harris have established their own value creation monopoly in the education industry.

Here is how we define this term: *A value creation monopoly is the permanent and practical ownership of a market niche that no competitor can comprehend or duplicate.* Tony and Mary Miller, over the years, have had many conversations with the owners of other janitorial companies, where these competitors ask how Jancoa is getting such extraordinary results. *"Even when we tell them in quite specific terms,"* Mary says, *"they don't seem to understand how we're doing it. Our success drives them a bit crazy, but so far they've shown no interest in learning from us."*

The monopoly is only possible with a Unique Process.
The reason there is no understanding or learning, I contend,
is that a value creation monopoly can only be established and
expanded by an entrepreneur who is operating inside of a
Unique Process. The competitors that Richard Rossi and Tony
and Mary face can only think in the conventional terms of their
industry. They don't think in terms of transforming situations,
nor do they think about having long-term creative relationships
with their clientele and employees.

The reason they don't is because they can't. Everything in
their commoditized world depends upon selling products
and services at a lower price than their competition. Every
business day is filled with dangers and frustrations. From this
perspective, their clients are adversaries who want to pay
them as little as possible, and their employees are liabilities
who want to work as little as possible. With this attitude,
those entrepreneurs who do not operate from within a Unique
Process cannot comprehend the growing success and satisfaction of those who do.

John Ferrell frequently meets intellectual property lawyers who
talk about being "burned out." He says, *"Most of my entrepreneurial clients are a treat. I love the new ideas, I love the work, I
love the creativity, and I love the progress they are making, the
big success stories. For these other lawyers who don't have a
process, it's all a grind after a while. They don't get the same
satisfaction. They have great skills, but they don't have a great
outlook."*

Giving new ideas and enterprises a fighting chance.
John Ferrell's comments here are particularly pertinent
because the very purpose of his Unique Process is to create
the legal protections that provide his entrepreneurial clientele with "marketplace monopolies." John says he thinks the

reason monopolies are so important for his clients is that most of them are startups without significant funds, infrastructure, or personnel. They're just getting started and trying to create a beachhead in industries where much larger organizations can outspend and outlast them, unless he gives them an advantage. That advantage comes in the form of patents, copyrights, trademarks, and trade secrets organized around their innovation: *"Once I help them create this protection, it gives them the solid platform and the time to develop into suc-cessful, profitable companies. Big corporations already have all sorts of advantages. I want my entrepreneurs to have some of their own."*

People I talk to about the subject of monopoly frequently have a negative response. They say things like, *"How can you believe in creativity, innovation, and entrepreneurism and think that monopolies are a good thing?"* My answer is that the kind of monopoly that Unique Process entrepreneurs create is operationally different from most of those in the world of government and corporate bureaucracies. Those are usually static monopolies in which nothing new is created. That's why I use the term "value creation" to differentiate the monopoly enjoyed by Unique Process entrepreneurs. These entrepreneurs achieve permanent, protected economic zones where they can continually create new solutions for their clientele's most pressing issues, without the competition being able to understand what is taking place.

The law ratifies a monopoly that already exists.
We strongly recommend that Strategic Coach clients take advantage of the full powers of intellectual property law in this endeavor. But the legal tools aren't actually what create and expand the value creation monopoly. All of the "ingredients" outlined in this book are the real building blocks. Overcoming adversity, passion, differentiation, value creation, transfor-

mation, bypass, and intellectual capital all enable Unique Process entrepreneurs to carve out their monopoly advantage. This advantage, once established, continually develops and expands. The use of legal tools then adds another layer of strength and legitimacy to the advantage that already exists.

Every entrepreneur would love to have the benefits that a value creation monopoly provides. In sports terms, it allows you to play offense, with minimum time and cost for defense. As it becomes known that you have this advantage in the marketplace, talent, resources, and opportunities continually flow to support it. All the examples of Unique Process entrepreneurs in this book point to very real value creation monopolies at work in the marketplace.

The final interview is with David Allen, who is perhaps the clearest example of a Unique Process transforming a whole industry. Because the private jet industry is relatively new, David has been able to create a global impact and reputation within five years of entering the market. His is a great story, and a perfect one to end this book.

David Allen

The Allen Groupe Experience™

David Allen approached the aircraft cleaning industry — one characterized by extreme complexity and ruled by safety issues that, understandably, underlie every situation — with a fully developed Unique Process, The Allen Groupe Experience™. With this as his foundation, David's business has not only experienced exponential growth over just five years — last year's figure was 325 percent — he sees a future of unlimited potential.

Dan Sullivan: Why don't we begin, David, with a little biographical information? Describe your first venture as an entrepreneur.
David Allen: Well, there's actually a fun story behind this. I grew up in Indianapolis, Indiana, right next to the Speedway racetrack. In high school I started cleaning cars to get some extra money on weekends and over the summer. Then my friend started a mobile detail car wash and we started washing all the transporters for the Indy car racing teams. It certainly wasn't your everyday car-washing job. Eventually, my friend, whose name is Mel Harder, went to work for the Indianapolis Motor Speedway, where he is now Senior VP of Operations.

Dan Sullivan: And you continued cleaning cars?
David Allen: Yes, I did. At this stage, I wasn't in the airplane-cleaning business yet. I was expanding my car detailing business. But I just kept hitting a ceiling, and I wasn't experiencing the breakthrough growth that I really desired.

Dan Sullivan: So what was your next step, David?
David Allen: That's when I came across your material, Dan. Believe it or not, I discovered your tapes in one of my client's cars. Because I was traveling to New York City the next day, I asked him if I could borrow his *How the Best Get Better* tape. Not only did he let me take it, he also gave me the Unique Ability

tape. So I listened to both tapes on the way to New York City, and I eventually transcribed them word for word. I was so interested in what you had to say, Dan, that I knew right then that I wanted to get the full Strategic Coach experience.

Dan Sullivan: *But first you had to qualify.*
David Allen: That's right. For the next four years I was focused on earning enough money to qualify for the Program. And it was during this time period that I began to get interested in aviation. Several of my car detailing clients owned private jets. I had the opportunity to clean them, which I really enjoyed. And I began to see a future in the aircraft detailing business.

Dan Sullivan: *Now, I'm sure that cleaning an airplane is a far more complex job than cleaning an automobile. So why don't you talk a little about that, David, because I'd expect the complexity of the business was a little daunting to you at these early stages.*
David Allen: You bet. There's a whole host of issues that comes along with aircraft cleaning, safety issues being the number one concern. You've got to be careful about the chemicals you employ. You can't use a pressure washer. There's equipment on the outside of the airplane that's related to the instruments of the airplane, so you can't damage or clog it. Again, it always comes back to safety. Aviation is the kind of business where everything impacts an aircraft's ability to get off the ground safely. You can have the best pilots and maintenance workers in the world, but a negligent cleaning person is a huge problem.

Dan Sullivan: *Did you have someone that sort of showed you the ropes early on?*
David Allen: Well, I was fortunate enough to have a friend whose company had three airplanes. One day he said, "Why

don't you come out and talk to our chief pilot, because I heard him complaining about cleaning?" So I went out, and this pilot, who was desperate for good cleaning, really showed me the ropes. I also made my own efforts to get educated. I attended a carpet-cleaning school. I went to a leather-cleaning school. I contacted the manufacturers of avionics and asked, "How do you want your avionics cleaned?" I really tried to zero in on each component of the aircraft and master the cleaning process.

Dan Sullivan: *Now, at this stage, you were still working on pretty small planes.*
David Allen: Yes. These were prop planes. And at that time, we were basically a three-man shop—me and two other team members. But from the beginning, we strived to be as professional as possible. We wore uniforms. We printed business cards. We sent professional invoices. We did everything necessary to start gaining credibility in the industry.

Dan Sullivan: *But you needed a breakthrough.*
David Allen: Exactly. And one day I got a phone call from NetJets, a Berkshire Hathaway company that provides fractional aircraft ownership. They were starting a cleaning department and doing vendor audits at all the airports in which they operated. Basically, nothing like this had ever been done before. They wanted to know what products you were using. They wanted access to your three-year business plan.

Dan Sullivan: *And they probably didn't expect to get an organized response from any of the cleaning companies.*
David Allen: You hit the nail on the head, Dan. The gentleman who created this document was essentially told by his superiors, "This is cleaning. You're not going to find anyone who runs their business like a business." After receiving my packet he called back and said, "I just want to let you know that this

■ *I knew I had to figure out how to have a cash flow breakthrough, and the only way to do that was through a Unique Process.* ■

is the most comprehensive, most complete vendor audit I have ever received." The reason I could respond in such a powerful fashion is because I had already done a lot of thinking in the Strategic Coach Program. Basically, I put to work a lot of the tools and concepts I was learning in the workshops.

Dan Sullivan: *That's great.*
David Allen: It sure was. And the relationship with NetJets just flourished from there.

Dan Sullivan: *Now at this time, were you still in Indianapolis?*
David Allen: Yes. When I began to work with the NetJets people, they gave me five or six cities to which I could relocate. I chose Orlando. So NetJets was my main customer, and they really provided a great foundation for my business to grow. While I've expanded into new areas, our relationship remains stronger than ever.

Dan Sullivan: *Was this a financial agreement or just a new opportunity?*
David Allen: An opportunity only, and that's the way I wanted it. You know, I've always had a "no entitlement" attitude. We're only as good as our last cleaning. I still bring that attitude to work every day.

Dan Sullivan: *When you first moved to Orlando, how many jets were you handling in a typical week?*

David Allen: It wasn't very many, maybe three or four per weekend. But I was basically working alone. And the cleaning process can be very labor intensive. You're talking about polishing the paint, deep cleaning the leather and carpet. For one plane you're talking about anywhere from eight man-hours to 30 man-hours.

Dan Sullivan: *Wow. So at what point did you begin to think in terms of "team."*
David Allen: Well, Dan, I was just destroying myself, medically speaking. After a series of surgeries on my elbows and other parts of the body, I finally came to recognize that "enough is enough." I was hitting a wall. It's that whole entrepreneurial cycle where you make ten dollars, and by the time you collect the ten, you've already spent fourteen. I knew I had to figure out how to have a cash flow breakthrough, and the only way to do that was through a Unique Process.

Dan Sullivan: *Let's talk about that, David. How did your Unique Process develop?*
David Allen: I took several key initiatives. First, I started to find more base customers located out in the field, unlike NetJets, where you never know when they're going to come in. I told them, "We'll manage the cleaning of your airplane. We'll just look at it on an annual basis. We'll give you a fixed budget and divide that by 12. You can prepay three months out and get the discount that you're looking for." They loved the idea. At the same time, we started to look for more locations where we could work with NetJets. We added Palm Beach, which is a great market. I mean, you've got people with very high net worth coming in there every weekend. I had much more exposure to people who were really hungry for good aircraft cleaning.

Dan Sullivan: *But you were able to capitalize on this market because you came at it with a clearly defined Unique Process.*

David Allen: That's correct.

Dan Sullivan: *David, I have a copy of your Unique Process, The Allen Groupe Experience™. Why don't you walk me through each of the five stages so people can get a sense of how your process is structured?*

David Allen: Sure. The first stage is called The Pre-Flight Discovery™. The Pre-Flight Discovery is an interview process that's based on The D.O.S. Conversation*. We have two types of questionnaires. One deals with budget, because it's very important to get the budget questions out of the way early on. Some clients come to us and say, "You just give us the number, and we'll do this as a traditional negotiation." And I have to tell them that if this is the process they want, then I'm not the right guy.

Dan Sullivan: *So what method do you use to close the deal?*

David Allen: Think about it this way, Dan. Let's say a client is ready to allocate one million dollars to airplane cleaning. We're going to take that number and divide it by the number of airplanes. Then we'll be able to tell the client how many times a year each airplane can be cleaned. In the vast majority of cases, the client will come back and say, "That's not enough. We want more cleanings." So they are essentially forced to go back to their CFO and their accountants and ask for more money.

Dan Sullivan: *You are basically turning the negotiation into an internal dialogue within the firm.*

David Allen: Exactly. And when they finally come back with a number, whatever it is, we can enter stage two of the process, The Flight Plan™. Here, we are basically doing what I already described above: taking the total budget number, dividing it by the number of airplanes, and making sure that the client is

*For the definition of The D.O.S. Coversation, please see page 212.

clear about the range and quantity of the different services he can expect.

Dan Sullivan: *Having that clarity upfront is great.*
David Allen: It really is. And we've also developed a tool that gives clients an even greater capacity to monitor the cleaning process. This tool represents the third stage of the process, which we call The Autopilot Navigator™. Basically, a company like NetJets has approximately 500 airplanes. At any one time, 75 to 100 airplanes will need some kind of cleaning. So the challenge we were facing was how to coordinate cleaning work with the aircraft maintenance work. And in this industry, maintenance always has priority over cleaning. If a plane is out of service for eight hours, and it takes six hours to maintenance the plane, then there really isn't any time left for cleaning.

Dan Sullivan: *You're the one getting squeezed.*
David Allen: Unfortunately, yes. I'm the one out of an opportunity. So I went to NetJets and said, "This doesn't work. You have hundreds of airplanes sitting on the tarmac at night when the pilots are sleeping. We can clean those airplanes when they're sitting on the ramp, and we won't bother anybody." With that in mind, I developed software that allows a company to instantly track their entire fleet. This software is web-enabled, so all the client has to do is log in, and their fleet automatically comes up. Once a plane has been cleaned, it disappears from the website. Then when a plane needs cleaning, it pops back on the list, along with the level of service required. So the cleaning department person at NetJets can go through the list every night and call his vendors, whether they're in Palm Beach, Las Vegas, or wherever.

Dan Sullivan: *In other words, this system works with any vendor. It benefits all of the cleaning companies.*

I look back to my early days in the industry. I was run-ning a three-man shop. Yet we had business cards. We had insurance. We had uniforms. I brought a college education to the table. So from the very beginning, our contrast with some of the mom-and-pop operations in the industry was very clear to clients.

David Allen: I've created a system that helps my competi-tion. I've created a system that helps everybody, because I'm not in every location. So it behooves me to be the Industry Transformer. It behooves me to be the trendsetter that people look up to, and that applies to the entire experience we provide for clients.

Dan Sullivan: The other thing, of course, is that this software program is laying the groundwork for you to go into all of those other cities.

David Allen: Exactly. We are continually looking for new loca-tions. And the reason we feel so confident is because our client experience really is unparalleled. That gets to the fourth stage, which we call The Allen Groupe Difference™. This is really about how we present ourselves—our uniforms, our aviation-approved products and techniques, our equipment—and how this gives our clients confidence that we really know what we're doing. We end the process in stage five with The Post-Flight Debrief™. Here, we review the entire "flight plan" and see if we need to adjust anything with the cleaning process.

Dan Sullivan: Why don't we take time here, David, and talk about some of the different ways that your client experience is unique in the industry?

David Allen: I'd love to do that, Dan, because I've always felt that we should be judged not just by the cleaning, but by the total quality of the experience we provide to clients. You know, I look back to my early days in the industry. I was running a three-man shop. Yet we had business cards. We had insurance. We had uniforms. I brought a college education to the table. So from the very beginning, our contrast with some of the mom-and-pop operations in the industry was very clear to clients. And, obviously, that's what helped us get the NetJets business.

Dan Sullivan: It's amazing how much impact things like uniforms can have on client perceptions.

David Allen: You're totally correct about that, Dan. I mean, our uniforms are Adidas CoolMax uniforms. Everything always looks new and nice. And these uniforms also give our team members a real sense of pride about the job at hand. The same can be said for our equipment. When the mechanics come in, they see our Honda generators. These are the same generators that the mechanics themselves are putting in the back of their cars and taking on camping trips. Not to mention that the Honda generator uses a small fraction of the fuel the typical home improvement center model uses. This generator pays for itself in a year.

Dan Sullivan: It must be difficult to impress mechanics.

David Allen: (Laughing) Dan, you're certainly right about that one. It gets back to my earlier point about the often adversarial relationship between cleaners and mechanics. We've just seen an unbelievable paradigm shift. When they're dealing with mechanics, I teach my team to say things like, "Excuse me, sir. Can I work around you and clean this wheel?" We work around them; they don't work around us. This ability to master the entire safety aspect of the job and work seamlessly with all the other aviation professionals is a key element of our client experience.

Dan Sullivan: *You're acquiring a very positive reputation.*
David Allen: It's humbling to us, and it's also empowering to the workers who are getting positive feedback.

Dan Sullivan: *Why don't you talk a little about the structure of your team?*
David Allen: First of all, I wouldn't be here if it were not for the support of my wife, Melissa. It was her income and effort that supported us during the early days. You always say that if you're going to succeed, you need to focus on your Unique Ability and then build a team around your weaknesses. Melissa really allowed that to happen by taking over the accounting, scheduling, and developing relationships with our existing clients.

Next, we focused on our infrastructure. This includes a CFO, COO, Director of Private Aviation, Director of Commercial Aviation, Director of International Operations, Manager of Human Resources, Manager of Information Resources, Manager of Special Events, Manager of Training, Western Regional Manager, Chief Pilot, and a Dream Manager. This gives us a Fortune 500 foundation to take advantage of the opportunities that exist globally. We have over 140 team members, but it's "bottom heavy," if I can use that term. All of the people who clean the planes have great pride and professionalism. We give them extensive job training, and we let them progress up the line from single-engine, to twin-engine, to light props, and then jets. It's a strict meritocracy. The better someone's performance, the more responsibilities he or she acquires, and the higher their pay. Eventually some of them become managers and team captains.

Dan Sullivan: *I'm sure that in the normal mom-and-pop business, there's tremendous turnover.*

David Allen: There sure is. And we have much lower turnover. I should also mention that we are actively working with Tony and Mary Miller to implement their Dream Manager program in our business. Since we're both in the cleaning industry, we face many of the same challenges and hold many of the same opportunities when it comes to our labor force.

Dan Sullivan: That's fantastic, David. I love to see this cross-fertilization between Unique Processes because that's what contributes to industry transformation.
David Allen: I agree.

Dan Sullivan: Let's talk about some numbers, David. So five years ago, you were making that NetJets connection and operating in Orlando. Now how many cities are we talking about?
David Allen: Five years later, and we've added 16 additional locations in the United States. We're also getting ready to open in Europe in Le Bourget, France; Luton in England; and also in Zurich.

Dan Sullivan: What's the potential moving forward in terms of new locations?
David Allen: I would say there's potential for 65 to 75 additional locations in the United States. The potential in Europe would be closer to 15. So that's all very exciting.

Dan Sullivan: You've also been contacted by some regional airlines who are becoming interested in your service, right?
David Allen: That's correct. We're just starting to explore this market.

Dan Sullivan: I'm sure you've experienced just phenomenal growth in terms of revenue and gross dollars.
David Allen: Well, as you know Dan, I struggled for several

Once they experience The Pre-Flight Discovery, once they go through The D.O.S. Conversation and complete our questionnaire, it's a done deal.

years just to qualify for your Program. When I started with you, our sales were around $100,000. That was seven years ago. Now our growth percentages over the last three years are 68 percent, 86 percent, and 325 percent.

Dan Sullivan: *With almost unlimited potential.*
David Allen: That's right. We've barely scratched the surface.

Dan Sullivan: *That's all very exciting, David. And what's so impressive to me is that you've gone into an area that historically has not earned very much respect in the aviation world. And you've totally transformed people's perceptions of the kind of experience they can expect from an aircraft cleaning company.*
David Allen: Thank you for the kind words, Dan. You know, I like to tell people about an advertisement that we put in a major business aviation trade magazine. The ad begins by asking, "Did you get into aviation to clean airplanes?" And, of course, the response for most readers is visceral. Nobody gets into this business to clean airplanes. Yet once you become the chief pilot or the director of maintenance or the director of the flight department, you're responsible for the cleaning. You take the fall if some aircraft cleaner doesn't show up and do his job. So the advertisement says, "Did you get into aviation to clean airplanes?" And right underneath it says, "We did."

People love that ad because it really taps into their emotions.

Nobody wants to manage the cleaning, and nobody knows how to do it. The chief mechanic doesn't. The director of maintenance doesn't. Nobody knows how to deal with the paint, the carpets, the leather, and the windows. For example, carpets on airplanes can cost you anywhere between $15,000 and $100,000 to replace, because they have to be certified and burn-tested. Paying a little extra for a cleaner who won't damage your carpets looks like a no-brainer now, doesn't it?

Dan Sullivan: *We're talking about big investments on these planes.*

David Allen: Exactly. And I need to be able to clearly communicate my value proposition to clients. So that's where the Unique Process comes in. Once they experience The Pre-Flight Discovery, once they go through The D.O.S. Conversation® and complete our questionnaire, it's a done deal. They're actually thinking, "Hey, this is too good to be true." I constantly have people come up to me and say things like, "What I love about doing business with you is that we delegate the task and forget about it. We don't have to think about it or manage it. It's as good as gold. It's freedom."

Dan Sullivan: *Let's talk a little about David Allen. You've really undergone a remarkable transition from operating essentially like an hourly worker, to running a budding empire. What's really special is that not only have you created a great company, you're starting to create a great industry. What have the last few years meant for you on both a personal and professional level?*

David Allen: It's really been an amazing experience for both Melissa and me. We are very humbled by everything that's happened. It often occurs to me that the difference between good and great might only be that extra five percent. But so many people miss the mark. They're so close, yet so far away.

And I think what's been important for me is just having faith and confidence that you can build a better mousetrap, so to speak. On a personal level, what this has done for me as a father, as a husband, and as a friend to so many other people is just tremendous. I am so fortunate to be living this dream. Aviation and entrepreneurship are both passions, and to be able to blend both is extremely rewarding. Melissa and I will be forever grateful that Strategic Coach gave us the tools to make that a reality. I remind others that the most powerful machine in the world is a locomotive, but it has absolutely no value unless it is on a set of tracks.

For contact details on The Allen Groupe Experience, please see page 213.

The Best Of All
Entrepreneurial Worlds

Afterword
The best of all entrepreneurial worlds.

Lately, it has occurred to me that I live a charmed life because of the many successful entrepreneurs I know. Every day I am in the presence of individuals whose lives and work combine extraordinary integrity, optimism, imagination, creativity, commitment, and value creation. The experience makes me happy to be alive. When I think of the nine entrepreneurs featured in this book, I always see them as having futures that are much bigger than their pasts. As successful and useful as they already are, the best part of their lives lies ahead. Each of them thrives on change, challenge, possibility, and opportunity. Each of them is passionate about making the world a better place than he or she found it. All of them measure their personal progress in terms of how much they contribute. They measure their professional success in terms of how much they have transformed the lives and conditions of other people. Being surrounded by these outstanding entrepreneurs, then, makes it much easier for me to aspire to the same qualities and results in my own life and business.

Making life more successful and enjoyable for others.
John Ferrell, when I asked what motivates him, said, *"I love entrepreneurs. I love the way they think, the way they create, and the way they are willing to risk their money, their security, and their reputations to create something new, better, and more useful in the world. I want to use my legal skills in the best*

possible way to help them protect what they create, and to make it possible for them to be richly rewarded for their innovations."

John's comments are typical of the spirit that motivates all the Industry Transformers in this book, and the many others who are in Strategic Coach. They all want to make life more successful, enjoyable, meaningful, and rewarding for other people.

Don Munce is equally passionate when he talks about linking up millions of graduating high school students with the colleges and universities that will be best for them. Richard Rossi is passionate when he describes how his company enables the best and brightest students from around the world to get in touch with their best abilities and opportunities.

Because I spend hours conversing with these Industry Transformers, it makes it very easy to be optimistic about my own future. It is also easy to be optimistic about the futures of many other people. As a result of the work that all of these individuals are doing, and because of the significant impact that their Unique Processes are having, the world is becoming a better place to live and work in for millions of other people. And in the case of each of these Industry Transformers, he or she considers what has been accomplished so far as a very small beginning.

Finding gold mines where others see nothing of interest.
David Allen sees a huge future for himself, his company, and his clientele: *"So far, we have only scratched the surface. Right now, we are only at the beginning of professional aircraft cleaning for private jet travel. Within ten years, the industry worldwide will double in the number of aircraft and people involved. Every one of these jets will need what we offer. All of these new owners will be looking for the peace of mind that comes from using our Unique Process. And as good as we are now, we are still adding*

new levels of service and support to what is acknowledged as the best detailing approach in the world."

One of the interesting aspects of the stories we've told in this book is that three of the examples come from an industry that many people think is mundane and unattractive: *cleaning.* Joe Polish with carpet cleaning, Tony and Mary Miller with janitorial services, and David Allen with the cleaning and detailing of private jets, are all in businesses that most people would describe as "dead end." After all, how much creativity, reward, opportunity, and satisfaction can there be in never-ending worlds of cleaning up other people's messes? It's a very good question, and the answer is "not very much" if you are approaching these businesses in a conventional, commoditized way. These truly are dead-end businesses when they are operated by people with dead-end ideas and methods. They are very definitely dead-end occupations when they are performed by individuals with dead-end attitudes, capabilities, and aspirations. Yet to listen to the interviews with Joe, Tony, Mary, and David, you'd think they had all discovered gold mines. And they have. They've discovered an economic secret, more valuable than gold, about what makes all work and all areas of life interesting and stimulating in the 21st century: *understanding the emerging needs, desires, and wants of clientele, and then creatively transforming these issues into new forms of service and support that provide the clientele with a greater sense of control over their future.*

It doesn't matter that the business and activity in these three examples involves cleaning. What really matters is that all of the clients and customers of these three Industry Transformers feel more confident about their futures. There's a whole part of their lives that is now handled in a way that will always give them peace of mind. There's a whole area of worry, frustration, and annoyance that now gives them a sense of confidence and capability.

This process of understanding and transformation is not just done once, but continually. It is not done as a one-time transaction, but as part of an ongoing creative relationship with clients and customers that continually improves. Gary Boomer, who started his professional career as an accountant, talks about the difference that the Unique Process makes: *"Ask the average person his opinion of accounting, and he will say it's boring—and the same goes for the accountants who do it. I have to agree. When I was an accountant, much of the work was boring, but now I know that it is the accounting profession that makes it that way. It's reactive and backward-looking. Since I created my Unique Process, the work has become increasingly exciting for me. We've taken a boring occupation and made it creative and proactive. And all of the accountants who use our process start to see their work as stimulating and creative, as do their own clients and customers."*

Philip Tirone reports the same change in his mortgage business: *"Obviously, the mortgage industry is going through severe changes. Even during good times, the mortgage business is not the most exciting to be in. 7 Steps to a 720 Credit Score empowers the 50 percent of Americans with a credit score under 720 to change their credit score, which will change their life. Most people think that they are stuck with their credit score, which is not the case! I'm excited that my Unique Process can help people improve their life and, at the same time, make my work so much more enjoyable!"*

Transforming lives and society.
Philip's last statement, about changing people's lives for the better and about making a societal difference, is probably the biggest difference that a Unique Process approach makes to the thinking and performance of an entrepreneur. This sense that they are doing "big stuff" is what makes the Industry

Transformers so different from their competition. It's their sense that they are transforming the world around them that enables these Unique Process entrepreneurs to turn their occupations and activities into exciting sectors of the economy. The Unique Process approach says that there are no bad or boring jobs if they produce new kinds of value for clients. It says that absolutely any human activity or circumstance can be transformed into greater productivity and promise.

The big picture: Unique Processing the world.
At Strategic Coach, we have been developing both the concept and methodology of the Unique Process for the past 25 years. The first Unique Process was Strategic Coach itself, which has become the world's leading entrepreneurial coaching program. Over the years, we began to see that our underlying structure and model was transferable to every other kind of business. Our clients began to see that the way we organized and operated our business was the way they also wanted to organize theirs. Businesses from 60 different industries are represented in the Program, and all of them are able to adapt the Unique Process approach to transform their challenges and opportunities.

Over the last ten years, well over a thousand entrepreneurs have created Unique Process businesses that are thriving in ways not possible for them when they were commodity-based. Not only have their revenues and profits grown, they have also become increasingly immune to competition. Not only have their support teams and clientele improved dramatically, they have become immune to being commoditized. Their sense of personal direction, confidence, and capability has soared. As all of these improvements have occurred, these entrepreneurs have come to be seen as transformers in their industries. They are pioneering new concepts, tools, and systems that consumers love. Their more enlightened competitors come to them for guidance, hoping to become their students and customers.

In the early 21st century, we live in a general condition that is both scary and exciting. It is scary because it looks as if many of the large bureaucratic structures that were the bedrock of security for economic life are not dependable. This is true in both government and corporations. The introduction of microtechnology has brought with it a degree of rapid change and complexity that undermines bureaucratic approaches and methods. As a result, consumers in all sectors have become increasingly disappointed, frustrated, and angered by the treatment they receive from these large institutions. Shoshana Zuboff and James Maxmin in their book *The Support Economy* say that consumers in all sectors are looking for a new kind of "deep support" that provides them with a sense that they are in control. This is exactly how clientele feel when they experience the Unique Processes created by the entrepreneurs featured in this book. Clientele feel that they are more in control of their present conditions and future prospects. Our goal at Strategic Coach is to teach tens of thousands of entrepreneurs how to transform their businesses into Unique Processes so the reality of deep support spreads throughout all sectors of the economy and society. This is an exciting possibility that the 21st century offers.

In closing, I leave the final words to Tony and Mary Miller: *"We started on this path by trying to transform our business for ourselves, but it required that we transform things for our employees and our customers. When we saw what we had done, it became obvious that this transformation could go way beyond our own company. We've been at this for years, but it seems like we've just started. What lies ahead is incomparably more exciting than what lies behind."*

Glossary
Contact Information
The Strategic Coach Program
Acknowledgements

Glossary

The Ceiling of Complexity™. All growth in a company occurs in stages. With each stage, and the complexity that it brings, a point is reached where growth becomes impossible with the existing knowledge, skills, and capabilities. Working harder and longer in the existing stage no longer works; in fact, it is counterproductive. This point is called The Ceiling of Complexity. To break through this Ceiling, different strategies are needed to achieve a new state of simplicity in thinking, communicating, and performing.

Coach2®. An advanced level within the Strategic Coach Program, in which entrepreneurs continually transform their companies on the basis of the accelerating development and distribution of intellectual capital. Entrepreneurs at this level all have developed Unique Processes they are charging for in the marketplace. As a result, they increase their competitive advantage within their industry and are seen as the dominant innovator. *(The Coach2 program was discontinued in 2012. Currently, our high level program is The 10x Program™.)*

D.O.S.™ D.O.S. is an acronym for Dangers (D), Opportunities (O), and Strengths (S). By focusing on these three areas, it is possible to transform any prospect, client, or other important relationship by helping the other person eliminate their dangers, capture their opportunities, and maximize their strengths in order to reach their goals.

The D.O.S. Conversation®. This is a simple and highly effective way to quickly establish a relationship based on value creation. It gives you the crucial information you need to determine if and how you can provide direction, confidence, and capability to a prospect, client, or other key relationship. By focusing on the other person's dangers, opportunities, and strengths (D.O.S.), you create immediate value, clearly differentiate yourself from the competition, and revolutionize the way you develop long-term relationships with your clients and customers.

The Strategy Circle®. A problem-solving and planning tool for producing dramatic results. When presented with a goal, the brain naturally responds with obstacles that oppose this vision. The Strategy Circle uses this information to create the strategies necessary to achieve the goal.

Unique Ability®. A central concept of the Strategic Coach Program, Unique Ability is the essence of what you love to do and do best. These are a few characteristics of Unique Ability: It's a superior skill that others value; you love using it; it is energizing both to you and to others; and there is never-ending improvement. People who identify their Unique Ability have an extraordinary competitive advantage in any situation—but especially among those who are entrepreneurs. In Strategic Coach, entrepreneurs learn how to focus on just their Unique Ability activities and delegate everything else.

Unique Ability® Team. In order to focus on your most important Unique Ability activities, you need to be supported by people who have capabilities in areas where you don't. These other abilities free you up and allow you to do only those activities that produce the greatest results for the business.

Contact Information

■ **David Allen** · *The Allen Groupe Difference*[TM]

The Allen Groupe
4215 Lindy Circle
Orlando FL, 32827

Tel. 407.825.6910

Email david.allen@allengroupe.com
Website *www.allengroupe.com*

■ **Gary Boomer** · *The Boomer Technology Circles*[TM]

Boomer Consulting, Inc.
610 Humboldt Street
Manhattan, Kansas 66502.6035

Tel. Toll Free 888.266.6375 or 785.537.2358
Fax 785.537.4545

Email Gary Boomer lgboomer@boomer.com or
Eric Hunt erich@boomer.com
Website *www.boomer.com*

John Ferrell · *Strategic IP Process*

Carr & Ferrell LLP
2200 Geng Road
Palo Alto, CA 94303

Tel. 650.812.3400
Fax 650.812.3444

Email jsferrell@carrferrell.com
Website *www.carrferrell.com*

Mary Miller & Tony Miller · *The Dream Manager*^{TM}

JANCOA® Janitorial Services
5235 Montgomery Road
Cincinnati Ohio, 45212

Tel. 513.351.7200
Fax 513.458.3785

Email jancoa@jancoa.com
Website *www.jancoa.com*

Floyd Consulting Inc. (The Dream Manager)
1235A North Clybourn, #109
Chicago, Il 60610

Tel. 312-698-5025

Email dbrunnert@floydconsulting.com
Website *www.thedreammanager.com*

Don Munce · *Creating A Brighter Future For America's Youth*

National Research Center for College & University
Admissions
3651 NE Ralph Powell Road
Lee's Summit, MO 64064

Tel. 816.525.2201

Website *www.nrccua.org*

Joe Polish · *Piranha Marketing*™

Piranha Marketing, Inc.
4440 S. Rural Road Building F
Tempe, AZ 85282

Tel. 480.858.0008
Fax 480.858.0004

Website *www.joepolish.com*

Richard Rossi · *The Lifetime Advantage*™

Envision EMI
1919 Gallows Road
Suite 700
Vienna, VA 22182

Tel. 703.584.9200

Email envision@envisionemi.com
Website *www.envisionemi.com*

Philip Tirone · *7 Steps to a 720® Credit Score*

7 Steps to a 720® Credit Score
11400 West Olympic Blvd.
Suite 450
Los Angeles CA, 90064

Tel. Toll Free 877.720.SCORE
or 310.453.1901
Fax 310.453.1910

Website *www.7stepsto720.com*

The Strategic
Coach® Program

Dan Sullivan is known throughout the world as an innovator and visionary whose ideas have set the standard for others in the entrepreneurial coaching industry. The Strategic Coach Program, co-founded in 1989 with his wife and partner, Babs Smith, was the first coaching program exclusively for entrepreneurs, and remains the most innovative in terms of its ability to help participants make successive quantum leaps toward increasingly greater personal and professional goals.

Strategic Coach clients today not only significantly increase their income and free time, they build strong, future-focused companies that leave their competition behind. Many have set new standards in their industries and made significant contributions to their communities through the increased focus, resources, and creativity gained by participating in the Program. Because of these results in all areas of life, most participants continue year after year. They comment that, as their dreams grow, the Program grows with them.

The Strategic Coach Inc.
Strategic Coach is an organization created by entrepreneurs, for entrepreneurs. The company operates using the same philosophy, tools, and concepts taught in the Strategic Coach Program, and has grown more than ten times in the past eight years. With over 100 entrepreneurially-minded team members

and three offices—one in Toronto, one in Chicago, and one in the U.K.—the company continues to grow and enrich its offerings to an expanding global client base. Currently, over 3,000 successful and highly motivated entrepreneurs from over 60 industries and a dozen countries attend Strategic Coach workshops on a quarterly basis.

If you would like more information about Strategic Coach, its programs for entrepreneurs at all levels of success, or its many products for entrepreneurial thinkers, please call **416.531.7399** or **1.800.387.3206**. Or visit *www.strategiccoach.com*.

Acknowledgements

I would like to recognize and thank the many wonderful people who contributed their time and effort to the making of this book.

To the talented team of editors, Catherine Nomura, Myrna Nemirsky, and Kerri Morrison, thank you for all the hard work and dedication you put into making *Industry Transformers* the best it could be.

To the amazing designers, Suzanne Noga, Marilyn Luff, and Marvin Lam, thank you for the creativity and inspiration you provided throughout the process and for helping to express our ideas through your designs.

Thank you to Christine Nishino, Cathy Davis, and Moragh Cameron for lending us your expertise in coordinating all aspects of the printing for *Industry Transformers*. And to project manager Paul Hamilton for ensuring that the creative process was smooth, enjoyable, and on schedule.

And, finally, to our nine Industry Transformers, my appreciation for your ability to inspire us with your stories, and for allowing us to share your experiences and Unique Processes with others. Thank you to David Allen, Gary Boomer, John Ferrell, Mary Miller, Tony Miller, Don Munce, Joe Polish, Richard Rossi, and Philip Tirone for your generosity, enthusiasm, and teamwork in creating this book.